Fishguard Fiasco

Fishguard Fiasco

An account of the last invasion of Britain

by

John S. Kinross

Logaston Press

LOGASTON PRESS
Little Logaston Woonton Almeley
Herefordshire HR3 6QH
logastonpress.co.uk

First published 1974
This revised edition published by Logaston Press 2007
Copyright © John S. Kinross 2007
Copyright © illustrations as acknowledged, otherwise John S. Kinross

ISBN 978 1904396 68 0

Typeset by Logaston Press
and printed in Great Britain by
Oaklands Book Services, Gloucestershire

Cover illustrations by Ken Hutchinson

Contents

Pedair Hong ddaeth i mewn yn llawn
Tua Abergwaun ar un prynhawn,
Troisant gynta' dan Llanwnda
Lladd a lladrata llawer iawn

(Four ships came in a-laden
T'wards Fishguard one afternoon
They turned at first under Llanwnda
Killing and Plundering a-plenty)

Traditional verse about the Fishguard invasion
Translated by J.M.O. Jones

Acknowledgments

(to the First Edition, 1974)

There are many people I would like to thank for their help in writing this short account of the French invasion of Wales. Firstly Oliver Warner for his encouragement. Secondly the late J.B.H. Peel whose article in the Daily Telegraph Supplement first led me to the subject. Thirdly and most important of all to Lord and Lady Cawdor for their kindness.

I know of no historian dipping into Welsh history who has not owed a great debt to Major Francis Jones, C.V.O., T.D., D.L., M.A., F.S.A., Wales' Herald Extraordinary, and as part of this book was written in his office, my debt to him is greater than most.

Finally I would like to thank my correspondents in France, Charleston, South Carolina and elsewhere, particularly Mrs. B. Lefèvre, Dr. Peter Thomas, the late A.W.H. Pearsall, Mrs. Royston Brown, B.E. Howells, Major P. Howells, Lt. Cmdr. Burrington Harries, R.N. (rtd.), Mrs. A. Perkins, Mrs. G. Ehles, and most important of all, Mr. Wilfred Harrison, M.B.E., M.A., Curator of Tenby Museum, for reading the MS and making many suggestions and corrections.

(to the Second Edition, 2007)

The above acknowledgments still stand, but apologies if I have not acknowledged some persons as since deceased. The revised edition is due to Christopher Taylor of St. Davids and Andy Johnson of Logaston Press. Thanks also to the Secretary, Cawdor Castle, the staff of Carmarthen Museum, Charlotte New and colleagues of Pembrokeshire Museum Service and to Miss A. Walker M.B.E. of the Fishguard Invasion Centre Trust for their help with the illustrations, and to the staff of Tenby Museum.

Centenary and Bi-centenary Celebrations

The 1897 Centenary of the French Invasion was celebrated by a banquet — the Royal Oak in Fishguard still has the programme and menu on its wall — as well as a procession and the erection of a stone at Carregwastad Point. This can be reached from Llwanda church in about half an hour on a footpath that suddenly dips down to a stream and then climbs up sharply, so is unsuitable for the disabled walker.

In 1997 Elizabeth Cramp, R.W.S., designed a 100-foot long tapestry (see overleaf) which was made by a team of 76 stitchers and was the legacy of a bicentenary year of community events in Goodwick, Pencaer and Fishguard. The tapestry was exhibited for four years at St. Mary's Church Hall, but a more permanent home has been planned inside the Market and Town Hall in a newly constructed Mezzanine Gallery due to open in 2007. Some of the money still has to be raised for this and the Fishguard Invasion Centre Trust Ltd., owners of the tapestry, has been set up as a charity for this purpose.

*Welsh women in their red cloaks and stove-pipe hats
march round Bigney Hill to look like guardsmen*

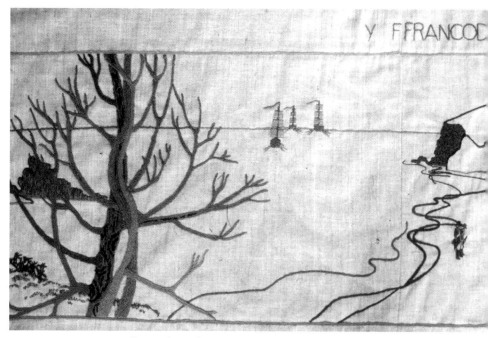

Scenes from the Last Invasion Tapestry

The French officers prepare to march to prison

The French surrender on Goodwick Sands
(all copyright Elizabeth Cramp)

Uniform of the Fishguard and Newport Volunteers c.1797
(Pembrokeshire Yeomanry Collection, Scolton Manor,
Pembrokeshire County Museum Service)

Prologue

The massive feeling of horror that greeted the news of the execution of Louis XVI on 21 January 1793 led Britain into the Revolutionary War. One man, William Pitt, tried every way to prevent the conflict. 'They will not accept,' he told the Commons, 'under the name of liberty, any model of government but that which is comfortable to their own opinions and ideas ... whatever may be our wishes for peace, the final issue must be war.'[1]

The threat to Holland was possibly the real cause but many, like Fox and his supporters, were still pro-France and did not consider the reasons for mobilisation in a period of bad harvest strong enough. The army consisted of no more than 15,000 men, excluding the 30,000 regulars scattered all over the British dominions. The Elector of Hanover provided a further 14,000 and the Prince of Hesse some 8,000. The navy, the first line of defence, had been well looked after by Sir Charles Middleton since the American Revolution and consisted of 113 ships of the line compared with France's 76. The weight of a British broadside was heavier than a French one but by 1796 the addition of the Spanish fleet to France was a serious threat and invasion as great a possibility as it was to be 144 years later.

At first the allied armies were moderately successful. The French General Doumouriez, victor of Jemappes, deserted to the Austrian camp and Mainz was captured. The Allies soon squabbled, however, and the French found a capable military organiser in Carnot, whose Committee of Public Safety in Paris began to run the French army on modern lines with proper transport, stores and supplies. In 1794 Lord Howe won the Battle of the Glorious First of June, defeating the French Admiral Villaret Joyeuse, but the latter's ships had been protecting a grain convoy from America and during the confusion the convoy slipped safely into Brest.

The earlier French disaster at Toulon, when Hood's force set fire to the arsenal and most of the French ships in the harbour, had been turned into victory for them, largely due to the hard work of a young artillery officer from Corsica, Napoleon Bonaparte, and in April 1795 the British army in the Low Countries was finally withdrawn. Prussia made peace with France and in May 1795 the Dutch fleet was annexed to that of the French. The wealth of Amsterdam was now at the disposal of Carnot and his ever greedy coffers. In England poverty in the lower classes increased so sharply that bread was almost beyond the reach of the labourers. By July 1795 the price of a quartern loaf was a shilling. The London Corresponding Society had already held a mass meeting in January 1794 to protest against the war and rising prices. The arrest of their secretary, Hardy, and two of his colleagues and their subsequent acquittal on a charge of High Treason did not lessen the anti-war feeling. On his way to open Parliament in October 1795 the king was greeted with shouts of 'Bread, No War, No Pitt' by an angry crowd and one of his coach windows was broken by a bullet from an early type of air-gun. New Acts forbidding political gatherings of more than 50 people were passed so that the Corresponding Societies soon began to lose both members and financial support.

In Wales the French could well imagine they might have supporters. Poverty was rampant and many large landowners were nonresident so that their wealth was taken out of the districts in which it was obtained. However, politically speaking, the Welsh speaking public depended on their church or chapel, their educational system and pamphlets for news. Pembrokeshire was probably more isolated than most of Wales, but it had some remarkable landowners.

The growth of education in West Wales owed a great deal to the hard work of the Philipps family of Picton. In 1699 Sir John Philipps had been one of the founders of the Society for the Promotion of Christian Knowledge which was concerned that the Welsh clergy were too poor to buy books and, as a result, education was being neglected. Libraries and schools were set up but Philipps withdrew his support when there was conflict between Methodists, whom he supported, and Anglicans, whom he mixed with socially. Farmers were also reluctant to support the schools when their children could be working in the fields helping with the harvest in summer.

The Methodists got round this problem by starting the circulating schools. Well organised by Griffith Jones, one of their leaders, they taught reading and the catechism and moved from one place to another every two or three months. The Anglicans naturally distrusted the Methodist schoolmasters and in the north they were so unpopular that Peter Williams, a circulating teacher, was locked in a dog kennel by Sir Watkin Williams Wynn.

Thomas Charles of Llanddowror, influenced by Griffith Jones, set up twenty circulating schools in north Wales and then started Sunday Schools for both adults and children. His example was followed by other denominations and the Methodists had their own Bible dictionary and catechism and a Bible commentary written by Peter Williams.

The pamphleteers took advantage of the new reading public.[2] Dr. Price, a Londoner and friend of Benjamin Franklyn, believed the Americans were fighting for liberty and defended their cause in his *Observations on the Nature of Civil Liberty*, which sold 60,000 copies and was followed by a sermon on the *Love of Country*, which claimed that the king was subservient to the people. This was a great success in France. Price died in 1791 but his work was carried on by David Williams, a Chelsea schoolmaster and preacher, who went to France and became an honorary French citizen. His *Letters on Political Liberty* advocated annual parliaments, freedom of the press and ballots. As Price and Williams wrote in English their influence in Wales was small but the Glamorgan bard, Edward Williams, known as 'Iolo', wrote pamphlets in the Welsh language which were witty but lacked the inspiration of Price and Williams. He was a leading member of the Gwyneddigion, a London Welsh society that encouraged Welsh drama and music as well as being political in nature. It brought back the eisteddfod and distributed medals for successful bards. In 1790 one of these medals, now in the National Museum of Wales, had 'Liberty slays Tyranny' engraved on it and was designed by the French engraver Dupré. No doubt its creator made its cause known to the leaders of the Directory.

In 1791 the London Welsh Society was formed and it was their spokesman, Morgan Rhys, who produced the first political paper in Welsh, the *Y Cylchgrawn Cymraeg*. Rhys tried to take Bibles to France before the war started but, running out of funds, he came home disillusioned with the French and later emigrated to America.

In Carmarthen the Rev. Thomas Evans was put in the pillory for writing

And when upon the British shore
The thundering guns of France shall roar
Vile George shall trembling stand
Or flee his native land
With terror and appal.[3]

Perhaps the best seller of all political books was the *Rights of Man*. Thomas Paine, a Thetford corset-maker, was in a French prison in 1797 but his policy that every man should be able to decide his own future depending on his environment was as well known in Wales, as it was in America and France. 'Never did so great an opportunity offer itself to England and to all Europe as is produced by the Revolutions of America and France,' he wrote, 'By the former freedom has a natural champion in the Western world and by the latter in Europe.'

The French did not have any scheme for attacking England until the advent of Hoche. The young sergeant who led the attack on the Bastille, Louis Lazare Hoche, was now a general and in 1796 took command of the Army of the North. Before taking command he had to deal with the Royalist rising at Quiberon.

A motley force of French emigrés and British marines under Count Puisaye landed at Quiberon in June 1795. It was backed up by Admiral Warren's fleet, but all it succeeded in doing was freeing 600 Republican prisoners. Hoche watched the disembarking of a vast quantity of stores and ammunition. On the night of 19 July his men entered the Royalist stronghold at night and, unable to tell friend from foe, Puisaye's men fled in alarm to the British fleet. With the help of the marines some of the Royalist force was rescued but all the stores fell into Hoche's hands, and the General was not the sort of man to waste them. The Secretary at War, William Windham, anxious to please the war party in the Commons, produced another scheme out of his hat. Lord Moira was ordered to seize Noirmoutier Island, off the mouth of the Loire, and, when he declined, a force under General Doyle was sent out to support the Count of Artois and the remaining Royalists. They landed on Yeu island and soon ran out of supplies and had to be shipped home. It was a feeble attempt, which satisfied no one, least of all the Royalists.

Hoche now played his master-stroke. In Brest he had met young Wolfe Tone, who had convinced him that the only way to attack Britain was to land a French army in Ireland where they could be sure of support from Tone's United Irishmen. The business of raising a fleet, stores and storeships and organising an invading army of 15,000 men took the best part of a year and it was not until December 1796 that Hoche's squadron, commanded by the aged Admiral Morard de Galles, was ready to sail.

In the channel Admiral Colpoys' blockading squadron was too far away to intervene. The weather was bad and the rest of the channel fleet was in harbour with the exception of Captain Pellew's *Indefatigable*, a 44-gun frigate and its smaller sister the *Amazon*, of 36 guns. These two made such a commotion on the night of 15 December when the French left Brest by firing rockets, shining lights and firing their cannon, that the next morning daylight revealed that the *Seduisant* was on the rocks and two other French ships had collided.

The French fleet was scattered by the bad weather and the *Fraternité*, with Hoche and the Admiral on board, separated from the rest. On the 22nd most of them arrived off the Irish coast and attempted to beat up the length of Bantry Bay. Bouvet on the *Droits de L'Homme* took command in the absence of Hoche. He was probably never very keen on the project from the start and when the wind rose he gave the order to return to France. On board his ship, Humbert, a young French army officer, was raging at the wasted opportunity. There was no British fleet attacking them and only the weather prevented their landing.

Pellew, however, had the last word. He caught up with the *Droits de L'Homme* and, although outgunned, kept raking her with broadsides until she ran aground with great loss of life. The channel fleet under Lord Bridport, brother of Admiral Hood, set out too late and contributed nothing to the failure of Hoche's expedition. In Ireland 2,000 troops and two guns at Cork, where Admiral Kingsmill had a small squadron of six ships and a newly raised Militia of doubtful value, were the only objects in the way of Hoche's army. Wolfe Tone was to try again but by then it was too late. The French, however, had discovered that the way to England was via Ireland and across the Irish sea.

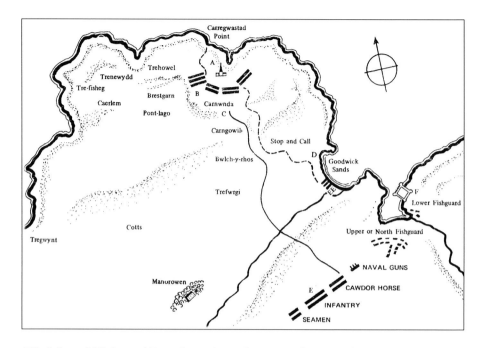

The Map of Fishguard Bay above shows the approach of Lord Cawdor's force to the French encampment on the night of 22 February, 1797.

   A.   *Llanwnda church where the French landed*
   B.   *Carnwnda, behind which the enemy took their station.*
   C.   *The British line of march the first night, but finding the enemy too numerous, returned to Station E*
   D.   *Goodwick village*
   EE.   *The second day's position*
   F.   *Fishguard Fort*

The dotted lines denote the march of the enemy down to Goodwick Sands where they piled their arms and surrendered themselves as prisoners.

1 The Militia

'To place any dependence upon Militia is surely
resting upon a broken staff' George Washington

The land defence of the British Isles at the start of the Napoleonic War
in 1793 rested almost entirely on the militia. There were regular troops in
barracks it is true, but detachments were constantly being sent to foreign
stations. The counties raised their own militia and Lord Strange's Bill of
1769 meant that they were fined if they failed to do so. By the end of
1794, 6,000 cavalry and 5,000 militia had been recruited on a voluntary
basis.[4] Only by passing the Supplementary Militia Bill two years later did
Pitt's government get the militia strength up to the quota of 60,000 for
England, 4,400 for Wales and 6,000 for Scotland. The cavalry, limited to
20,000 men, was to be raised by the method of every gentleman, if he
owned a stable of ten or more horses, supplying a horse and one man.
Gamekeepers were supposed to become sharpshooters and huntsmen
were often troop leaders. A militia man had certain privileges. He was
granted parish relief and a bounty of 6d. on joining and was supplied with
a uniform, both costly and elaborate.

In Pembrokeshire the Lord Lieutenant, Lord Milford, after a meeting
in London in 1794 with Lord Cawdor and other gentlemen of his county,
raised two troops of Gentlemen and Yeomanry cavalry, named Dungleddy
and Castlemartin troops after the hundreds in which they were raised.
Dungleddy is a version of the Welsh word Daugleddau, 'two swords',
and was an area between the two arms of the Cleddau but the word is
no longer in use. The Hundred of Castlemartin, the area between the
Haven and the south Pembrokeshire coast containing Stackpole Court
and Lord Cawdor's estate and the Hundred of Dungleddy were set up
in the sixteenth century under the Acts of Union between England and
Wales.

The men, fifty in each troop, were armed with swords and pistols and had twelve short carbines per troop. They wore white breeches, a leather helmet with moleskin turban and bearskin crest with a red and white plume. They had blue coats with buff collars, buff lapels and cuffs.[5] Each troop had a paid sergeant. The officers only received pay on active service, but the men drew pay for exercises. They were restricted to serving in Pembrokeshire but on occasions could go to the neighbouring counties of Carmarthenshire and Cardiganshire at the discretion of the Lord Lieutenant.

The Haverfordwest records show that Colonel Montrevor came to inspect the Pembrokeshire recruit situation in 1796. He asked the council when they would pay their fines. The Town Clerk said they would pay at once, having delayed his letter by a few days in case the required number of recruits should miraculously appear.

The forthcoming French invasion, however, was originally aimed at Bristol, not Wales and, unlikely though it was, in Buckinghamshire the force that was to defend Bristol was taking shape. The Marquis of Buckingham, a relation of Pitt and of other members of the government, decided that his militia should not only be the best equipped, but should play a prominent part in the military activities of the country. As an example of the sort of expense one man entered into for the sake of what was virtually his private army, Buckingham spent £564 7s. 6d. equipping his men. It was made up as follows:

	£	s	d
80 pistols from Mr. V. Walker of Suffolk Street	£372	14	4
12 carbines, scabbards, straps, swivels and accessories from Mr. Clark, 43 Holborn	33	16	6
73 bridles and goat skins from Philip Thomas of Hertford Street, Mayfair	62	0	0
8 swords, belts, goatskins holsters and pouches from Learmouth and Beazley	19	15	8
42 doz. buttons from Hawkes	3	19	6
27 uniforms from Christopher Irving of Marlow	72	1	6

On top of this was a total of £1170 7s. 0d. for the hatter who made hats for 440 men between 1794 and 1797.[6]

The militia took a long time proceeding from one place to another especially on the muddy, narrow winter roads but the trek of the Bucks Militia from Portsmouth to Bristol must have been really slow, even for

Quarter-Master Geest of the Pembrokeshire Regiment of Fencible Cavalry raised in 1795 and commanded by Lt. Col. Henry Davis. The Fencibles were both infantry and cavalry raised in the latter 18th century by private individuals for service under the Crown in the UK and Ireland. They were paid on the same basis as regular troops. This regiment was disbanded in Dublin in August 1800. The troops that served under Knox at Fishguard in 1797 are sometimes referred to as 'fencibles', but were, in fact, volunteer forces raised under different regulations (Pembrokeshire Yeomanry Collection, Scolton Manor, Pembrokeshire County Museum Service)

3

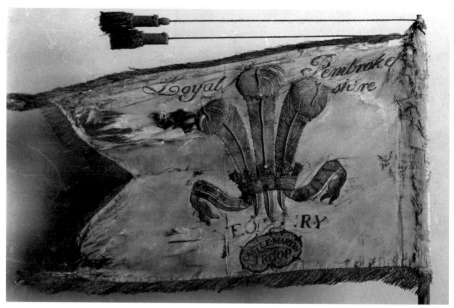

Standard of the Loyal Pembrokeshire Yeomanry, Castlemartin Troop, c.1803
(Pembrokeshire Yeomanry Collection, Scolton Manor,
Pembrokeshire County Museum Service)

those days. On 1 October they marched out of Portsmouth and covered a full ten miles to Fareham. This so wore them out that the next day was a rest day. On the 8th they reached Southampton, on the 9th Romsey, followed by another rest day on the 10th. On 6 October they reached Salisbury, the 7th Heytsbury and two days later Bath after a further rest day at Trowbridge. On the 11th some of the fitter ones reached Bristol where Private John Morris stole Private Allen's shoes as his own had been worn out in the march. He got off with a few lashes but Robert Pain, a constant troublemaker, had 100 lashes for stealing a shirt and selling his coat in January, and a further 120 a week later for selling two of his shirts.[7] The militia men were not fast marchers but they must have been hardy to go without extra clothing in winter.

Had the French suddenly landed at Bristol as Hoche originally planned, the militia there would have been unable to stop them. At the beginning of 1797 the second seaport in the country had no adequate defences.[8] There were small forts on the Bristol Channel islands but there was no naval base in the Channel and no militia. It was not until 18 February that the city officials held a meeting to form a Volunteer Regiment. In the chair was Evan Baillie, who appointed himself Lieutenant Colonel. The Lord

Lieutenant, the Earl of Berkeley, wrote to Baillie from Berkeley Castle, outside which he rarely went except for matters concerning the turf, saying that he had read the rules of the Yeomanry, which he approved, but he felt they should train men to work the field pieces. It was sound advice and the committee, consisting of Baillie, Lieutenant Colonel Gore, Major T. Kington and Major T. Haynes obtained the services of Major Worthington of the Sussex Militia to teach them the rudiments of gunnery.

The Regiment rules contained an elaborate system of fines. A man had to pay 5s. for absence from parade and 10s. for absence after receiving a warning. The fine for bad behaviour or rudeness to officers was not more than £2 2s. depending on the rank of the officer in question. The men came from all walks of life and included a pawnbroker, a rope-worker, a druggist, a tavern-keeper, a dry-salter, a clerk, a lime-burner, a brazier, a few hoopers and even a ferryman. Who ran the ferry when the latter was on parade for his weekly two hours we do not know.

The Volunteers did not reach their full strength until June when they consisted of '1,000 men, excluding 2 Lieutenant-Colonels, 2 Majors, 10 Captains, 10 Lieutenants, 10 Ensigns, 2 Adjutants, 1 Quarter Master, one Sergeant Major or as many men as required.'[9] On 9 June a great parade was held on Durdham Down and the new colours, embroidered by the good ladies of Bristol, were presented. There was a slight hitch in the proceedings when Colonel Baillie, deciding his daughter was too young to present the colours to her father, presented them to himself. Crowds waited for the start of the ceremony then suddenly dispersed at twelve o'clock when the rain came down heavily and 'threw a damp on the Glory of the Day.'

Baillie's men were not properly organised and the Bucks Militia could not have defended Bristol on their own. There was a spirit of keenness in the ranks, however, which made up to some extent for inexperience. Baillie's second-in-command was rudely interrupted during one parade by a choice comment from the rear rank: 'If you don't behave better, I'll raise your rent.'

The invasion, however, did not fall on Bristol. The two regiments of militia we are mainly concerned with here were defending Pembrokeshire. The Fishguard Fencibles — a fencible is a soldier enlisted for defence in time of war — were formed by William Knox, former Under Secretary of State in the American Colonies from 1770–1782 and recently retired to the Slebech and Llanstinan estates near Fishguard. He formed the Fencibles in 1793, putting his son, Thomas, who was in his twenties, in command. It was a very responsible post for such a youngster but by 1795 he had become a lieutenant-colonel and the reaction of those who considered that he should not be permitted such an exalted position was to dismiss the regiment and form their own — the Yeomen Cavalry.

The Fencibles were divided into two divisions, one under Knox, the other under Major Bowen. Their strength in 1797 was two captains, two lieutenants, two ensigns, six sergeants, six corporals, four drummers and four fifers and 235 ordinary fencibles. They wore striped jackets, slouch hats pinned on one side with a leek and the motto *Ich Dien* (I serve) on their ribbons. Only the colonel and the major had horses so the troop must have looked like Mexican gauchos without horses.

The Yeoman Cavalry wore busbys with white feather cockades, blue coatees with white cross straps and white breeches and black riding boots. They were few in number but very keen.

There is another militia force, the oldest in Pembrokeshire, which we must mention. The Pembrokeshire Militia, formed in 1780, was stationed at Landguard Fort, Felixstowe, where there had been a Dutch landing in 1667 that had been repulsed by the Earl of Suffolk in an action described by Pepys as the only success in a grim week when the Dutch entered the Medway and carried off some English capital ships. Their commander, Colonel Colby of Ffynone, was in Haverfordwest as he was also Governor of the town's castle. He was 46 and spent most of his time looking after his sister Lady Anne Owen's estate. He was a businessman with a town house in Haverfordwest as well as a new house at Ffynone. He had little time to give to the militia but was, nevertheless, a competent leader.

The real reason why the Government did not strengthen the coastal areas and cities like Bristol more effectively was probably because it believed the navy would halt any invasion fleet from France before they got their feet on British soil. Yet there were a few realists in the Government who were not too happy at the state of the navy.

In February 1797 the First Sea Lord, Earl Spencer, wrote a note to Lord Grenville, the Secretary of State for Foreign Affairs: 'The present state of the [blockading] force at Brest would admit of our so much weakening the channel fleet much battered by their late ineffectual cruise … I cannot help feeling of the great possibility of some other desperate attempt from Brest.'[10]

2 Fishguard

'Pencaer is a barrier thrown by the Ancient God across the path
of the Atlantic waves to prevent them separating the land from Fishguard.'
Isambard Kingdom Brunel

The creation of 'Little England Beyond Wales' goes back to Norman times.
The building of Pembroke and Haverfordwest castles guarded the sea
approach from England and the Norman settlers then constructed minor
castles at Roch, Wiston and Narberth to keep out Welsh invaders. Further
north there were castles at Cardigan, Cilgerran and Newport. The Bishop's
Palace at Llawhaden was also fortified. There was an artificial barrier or
Landsker across the county from Newgale to the Carmarthenshire border
near Narberth which is still today a language barrier.[11] A higher propor-
tion of people speak Welsh to the north of it than they do to the south.

The Pencaer peninsula is formed of igneous rocks of the ordovi-
cian period. Coves and bay have been formed by marine erosion on the
sedimentary rocks. The climate is surprisingly mild in winter and, even in
1797, the peninsula was dotted with isolated farms. Many, like Moor Farm
at Manorbier, which is outside the area but of the same period as some of
the Pencaer farms, were held by tenants as a reward for military service.

Fishguard was a small port, used for importing coal and culm for the
lime-kilns. It had a turnpike road to Haverfordwest and was also connected
to Cardigan. A series of narrow lanes connected the isolated farmhouses
on Pencaer. Llanwnda was the only hamlet with a church near the sea. It
is almost entirely surrounded by high rocks, the highest, Carnwnda, rising
500ft. above the church.

Benjamin Heath Malkin, whose book *The Scenery, Antiquities and
Biography of South Wales*, was published in 1807, was disgusted with
Fishguard. 'It is so ill built,' he wrote, 'as almost to be interesting on those
very accounts.' Carmarthen at this time had a water supply, paved streets

and even gas lighting but Fishguard 'is the only town I ever met with from which dunghills — I do not mean here heaps of dirt, but literal and *bona fide* dunghills — are not excluded.'

Peasants and small farmers worked round the clock on their small-holdings and there was no social gap between the two. The farm labourers might be hired for a year but were paid fortnightly. In Cardiganshire a labourer supplying his own food might earn sixpence a day but, if his employer supplied him with food, usually barley bread, buttermilk and potatoes, then this could reduce to as little as twopence a day. In south Pembrokeshire wages were usually better, but the women worked as hard or even harder than the men in supporting their families. Jemima Nicholas was the cobbler in Fishguard, a trade we might think unusual for a woman today, but it was not considered so in Wales at that time. Women wore a heavy cloth gown on their heads in the fields and on occasions a 'large beaver hat with broad brims flapping over their shoulders.' A church pamphlet of 1778 refers to the recent hideous fashion (*ffasin hyll*) of wearing tall stovepipe hats. This had replaced the beaver hat by Napoleonic times and in Fishguard the red whittle or shawl was a common sight.

Welsh women at market in the early eighteenth century

8

Fishguard in the early 19th century

Some women earned more than their husbands. One was 'taught by her mother to read and spin and she teaches girls the same … she can spin 2lb of coarse flax for ordinary sheeting and towelling at 2½d per pound, therefore supporting the business of the family to take up to two days in the week, the eight pounds spun in the other four days comes to 1s. 8d …. the little girl aged five can also spin adroitly, she goes to the wheat(fields) when her sister is otherwise employed.'[12] This family managed to earn £39 17s. 4d. in 1795, but their annual cost of living was £39 14s. 4d. which included items like 1s. 6d. for stockings, 4s. for shoes, 3s. 6d. for a shirt and other items of clothing. Most Pembrokeshire women at this time would make their own stockings, wigs and caps.

In Pencaer, until recent times, a farmer selling cattle or sheep, made it a practice to call at the kitchen first to deal with the wife of the household. Women often controlled the purse, supervised the labourers, managed the farm accounts and looked after the children while their husbands were out at market or working in some distant field. There was a great deal of bartering amongst farmers due mostly to the shortage of cash. Later the Welsh banks printed their own currency but by 1825 all the Pembrokeshire banks had closed in the depression that followed the rise in prices and rents that took place after the Napoleonic Wars.

Warner, who travelled in Pembrokeshire in 1798, said that at Christmas: 'the farmer pays off any little debt which his labourer may have contracted at the millers and presents him with three large loaves and two large wheaten loaves (each of about two gallons) together with a quarter of good mutton. This assisted the Pembrokeshire peasant, who brought to something like a rational level with his fellow creatures, perceives that he has a state in society and feels that the practice of certain duties result from this situation, all of which convictions operate upon him as powerful motives to decency and integrity, to cheerfulness and content. The cottages of this part … generally let at 15 or 18 shilling per annum each, having a small plot of ground attached to them which enables a tenant commonly to keep a pig and very often a cow.' Another traveller describes how the pig and the cow often shared the same room as the peasant, so Warner's observations are somewhat idealistic.

There were some enlightened employers. The Reverend Edward Hughes of Hafodonnen bought tobacco for all his harvesters as an inducement for them to return the following year. William Jones, a thresher, was paid £2 16s. for threshing oats in March and April 1797, and a similar sum in June and July for carting sand and lime. Many part-time labourers like Jones would work in the Pembrokeshire coal mines near Tenby and return to the farms when the weather improved. Lime-burning was a great industry for lime was in demand as a fertiliser. St. Clears was one of the many small ports where culm or anthracite coal would be brought by water to the kilns and the finished product carried in horse panniers many miles into the country. Some farmers collected their own lime, arriving at the toll gates at midnight and hoping to collect their loads and return before the following midnight to avoid paying a double toll. The toll roads were very unpopular and thirty years later the Rebecca Riots broke out in general protest against the greedy toll trusts and the social and economic conditions.

In Fishguard the American War of Independence had not gone unnoticed for a privateersman, believed by many to be John Paul Jones himself, had entered the harbour in 1779 and demanded a ransom of £500 for a merchant ship he had seized belonging to Samuel Fenton, brother of the local historian. A similar ransom was demanded from the upper town. Both were refused and the Dewsland Volunteers were summoned by Captain Harries of Crugglas but stood by while the ship fired on the town breaking a few chimney pots and injuring Mary Fenton (sister to Samuel and Richard), in the foot. Fortunately a local smuggler had placed his small boat in a cave near the harbour and opened up with his one cannon to such effect that the privateersman was driven off.

Stung by this insult to their security and, perhaps even more by the way the ship had been driven off by a local vagabond and not a member of the town council, the latter decided to build a fort. Gwynne Vaughan, who owned the land jutting out into the harbour off the Cardigan road, suggested this as the site and Sir Hugh Owen, Lord Lieutenant of the county at the time, supplied the finance. Colonel Knox describes it as 'in outline not very unlike a lady's fan when opened.' It had eight 9lb. cannon manned by three invalid gunners from Woolwich. It had, and still has, a strong barrel-roofed garrison room, no doubt used for quarters and perhaps for storing ammunition, of which there never seemed to be sufficient. Its one drawback was that it could not protect the upper town. Any ship entering Goodwick Bay and keeping to the Pencaer bank would be well out of range. If it moored near the Goodwick brook it would also be out of sight.

It is interesting to compare the Fishguard fort with the much more elaborate defensive arrangements in the Menai Straits. Fort Belan, built by Thomas Wynn, later Lord Newborough, still retains its 9lb. cannon and looks out over the southern tip of the straits and nearby, Fort Williamsburg is a garrison fort built inland with a strange belvedere for observation. Had the enemy landed here the troops at Williamsburg could be rushed to the necessary spot while the cannon from Belan held off the ships. Such a system would have worked well at Pencaer.

The Fishguard Fencibles were based at Gwynne Vaughan's Fort. They had been active in Haverfordwest in August 1795 when they defended a butter sloop which was threatened by a mob of rioting miners. They paraded every day for a week in the harbour — now Haverfordwest car park — and in the square on market days, and successfully prevented any serious riot. Corn dealers did not always get fair prices for their products that year due to the bad harvest. One ship put into Milford Haven and found the price of corn too low so set out for Cardigan. By the time it had arrived the word had reached Cardigan market that the price should be kept to the Milford figure so that the owner had to sell at this price. This is an example of how a message could get from one part of the coast to another without going by sea and arrive faster than it would have, had it been carried by ship.

The Landsker was not only a marker for language, it was approximately the dividing line between the advanced agricultural ideas of Lord Cawdor and other southern Pembrokeshire landowners and the primitive methods of the north. It was an old joke that northerners ate oats while southerners only gave them to their horses. Lord Cawdor inherited the Stackpole estate near Bosherston from his father Pryse Campbell in 1777 and it was 'one of the finest and best connected, all valuable land without the intervention of any mountain waste or common.'

The Castlemartin area, where the Cawdor estates were, was renowned for its black cattle. A Pembroke bull that sold for twelve guineas in 1794 could have reached twice that amount by 1802.[13] Lord Cawdor's oxen were renowned for their fast going and, amongst other improvements, he introduced the Suffolk punch into Pembrokeshire. He was a keen agriculturist and respected by the other landowners for his knowledge on the subject.

In spite of the varying military commands in Pembrokeshire — Knox's Fencibles, Lord Cawdor's Yeomanry Cavalry, Colonel Colby's militia, Captain Ackland's Pembroke Fencibles, the Cardiganshire Militia and the naval contingents of Captain Longcroft — the area was very cut off from London. Roads were frequently impassable and in winter fords would be flooded so that in 1791 a coach was swept into the Towy and its passengers drowned. It was at least a week's journey to London and the quickest method was by boat to Bristol, or the Somerset shore from Tenby or Swansea and then stagecoach to London. The traveller had to put up with major discomfort en route. 'Our apartment,' wrote a Mr. Barber about an inn near Fishguard, 'served not only for parlour and kitchen and hall but likewise for bedroom: everything was in unison, the discoloured state of the walls and furniture; the carefree look of our host and hostess, our scanty fare of barley bread and salt butter with nauseating ale … our bed a recess furnished with a bag of straw [in which] a legion of fleas attacked us at all points.'[14]

Shortly the people of Fishguard were to be attacked at all points by something larger and more deadly than fleas.

3   The French Plan

Tair blynedd cyn y deunaw cant
'Daeth y Ffrancod a'u holl chwant
Fn llabyddio a'n distrywio
Mynd a'n heiddo ffwrdd i bant

(Three years before 1800
The lusty Frenchies came
To kill us and destroy us
And take our property home)
Old Pembrokeshire verse. Translated by J.M.O. Jones

During the Jacobite insurrection of 1745 French privateers had helped the Scots by supplying their army with reinforcements. Bonnie Prince Charlie himself had been landed at Loch nan Uamh by a privateer captain and, sailing in pairs or singly, several French ships had slipped through the English fleet.

In 1756 a French privateer had attempted to land 200 men at Mounts Bay, Cornwall, but was driven off by a British ship. This was more an attempt to escape shipwreck than an invasion because of the gale-like conditions at the time.

The situation in Napoleonic times was similar. There were 95 privateers recorded in Boulogne between 1789 and 1815. These vessels were very fast as they could usually sail closer to the wind than English frigates. Their captains were given bounties according to the number of guns they carried, thus in 1809 one Boulogne ship had 14 cannon, 76 cannon balls, 10 canister shot, 7 blunderbusses, 40 muskets with 120lb. of bullets, 15 pistols and 30 sabres. Their crews would swarm on board English merchantmen and capture them, escaping at speed before the navy could intervene. Over 1,000 English ships were captured in this way in 1796 and 1797 alone.

One of the bolder captains, J.P. Antoine Duchenne, landed on the Sussex coast and stole some sheep to prove the superiority of English mutton over French in a wager he had with a colleague.[15] In 1794 a privateer caused a scare off the Northumberland coast. The Mayor of Newcastle received two letters signed by Henry Grey Bambourg and Thomas Younghusband Hall saying the French had landed in force and captured Bamburgh Castle. The Mayor called out the militia and there was an immediate panic, but the letter was found to be a hoax and a reward of £250 was offered for information about Bambourg and Hall.[16]

General Hoche planned an invasion of Ireland in 1796 and in December that year a fleet of 17 capital ships, many transports and frigates set sail from Brest under Admiral de Galles. Fortunately for Admiral Kingsmill, in command of the few British ships at Cork, the weather intervened and, although part of the French fleet entered Bantry Bay, the rest, including Hoche and his admiral, were driven out into the Atlantic. The opportunity passed and the French fleet struggled back to Brest, most of it unfit to set sail again for some time. However, the French fleet, guided by privateers, did manage to avoid any British ships.

As a result of the success in evading the British fleet the Directory planned two other invasions to take place shortly after the Bantry Bay expedition. To divert the British away from the south coast, a force, called the Legion Franche and commanded by General Quantin, was to attack Newcastle, burn the docks and shipping and escape in fast frigates. The Legion set out from Dunkirk in flat-bottomed barges in November and struggled round the coast as far as Flushing, where the bad weather forced the unseaworthy craft to founder. Some were wrecked on the way home and the Legion Franche, which consisted largely of criminals and deserters, rebelled against their officers and refused to re-embark.

Wolfe Tone, the inspiration behind the Bantry Bay expedition, had moved to Brest before the expedition set out and obtained a job as a translator at Hoche's headquarters, where he had a good friend in General Clarke, a fellow Irishman. It is from Tone's diary that we can follow the hectic days at Brest leading up to the third of Hoche's planned invasions, which was to be the only one to succeed in at least landing its force.

'I have been hard at work,' wrote Tone in his witty, informative style, 'half this day [24 November 1796] translating orders and instructions for a Colonel Tate, an American officer, who offered his services, and to whom the General has given the rank of Chef de Brigade, and 1,050

Brest: the embarkation point for Tate's troops

men of the Legion Noire in order to go on a buccaneering party into England. Excepting some little errors in the locality, which, after all may seem errors to me from my own ignorance, the instructions are incomparably well drawn; they are done, or at least corrected by the General himself and if Tate be a dashing fellow, with military talents, he may play the devil in England before he is caught.'

Two days later Tone had to alter part of the instructions when the destination was fixed at Bristol, instead of Liverpool as first contemplated. Tate was to burn it down, an act which outraged Tone's civilised mind. Discussing the plan with his friend Colonel Shee in a Brest inn, Tone thought of his wife and family, who were en route from America to Hamburg. 'I cannot but remark the misery the execution of the orders which I have transcribed and assisted in framing may produce ... the conflagration of a city as Bristol! It is no slight affair; thousands and thousands of families, if the attempt succeeds, will be reduced to beggary. I cannot help it! If it must be, it must, and I will never blame the French for any degree of misery which they may inflict on the people of England.'

Hoche's plans to Tate were as follows, (the original instructions were captured with Tate and subsequently translated at Whitehall):[17]

There will be placed under the command of Tate, a body of troops, completely organized, to the number of one thousand and fifty, all resolute determined men, with whom he may undertake anything: They are to be called La Seconde Legion des Francs.

The legion is completely armed; he will be likewise furnished with fast-going vessels with which he is to proceed, before, with, or after the squadron; the vessels will be victualled for the passage, but the legion will bring on shore nothing but their ammunition, which is to be musquet cartridges.

Col. Tate is to have the command in chief of the legion; the Admiral will give the necessary orders to the officer commanding the naval force, which will proceed up St. George's Channel ....

But should Col. Tate, on arriving opposite the mouth of the Severn, learn that the river is little or not at all defended and that the wind and tide allow him to sail up, he will endeavour to execute a coup de main on Bristol, which is the second city in England for riches and commerce; the destruction of Bristol is of the very first importance, and every possible effort should be made to accomplish it.

For this purpose, it will be proper to reconnoitre the mouth of the Severn, in the day time, and to sail up the Avon at night fall, within five miles of the town, where the landing should be made, on the right bank, in the greatest silence, and, the troops, being supplied with combustible matter, Col. Tate is to advance rapidly in the dark, on that side of Bristol which may be to windward, and immediately set fire to that quarter. If the enterprize be conducted with dexterity, it cannot fail to produce the total ruin of the town, the port, the docks and the vessels, and to strike terror and amazement into the very heart of the capital of England.

This object being fulfilled, Col. Tate will immediately reembark, cross the Severn, and land below Cardiff, which he will leave on his right, and proceed towards Chester and Liverpool, in the manner to be pointed out in these instructions.

During the passage, Col. Tate will take care that the troops observe the most exact discipline, and will recommend to the naval officers to carry a press of sail.

At the moment of the landing, each soldier is to be furnished with one hundred rounds of ammunition, provisions for four days, and a double ration of wine or brandy, to revive them after the fatigues of the voyage.

Not a moment is to be lost in the debarkation, and the soldiers must carry their ammunition and provisions until they can secure bât horses [ones used for carrying goods]; they are never to quit them, and are to take care to supply what may be expended on every possible occasion. For the first two days the legion is to keep in one body, observing not to suffer any to lag in the rear.

Col. Tate will feel the necessity of gaining a close and strong country with all possible speed, and before committing any act of hostility, he will take care to avoid the morasses, as well from regard to the health of the troops as to avoid being surrounded by the enemy, who would of course endeavour to profit of such a defect in his position.

The expedition under the command of Col. Tate has in view three principal objects: the first is, if possible to raise an insurrection in the country; the second is to interrupt and embarrass the commerce of the enemy; and the third is to prepare and facilitate the way for a descent by distracting the attention of the English government.

In all countries the poor are the class most prone to insurrection, and this disposition is to be forwarded by distributing money and drink; by inveighing against the government as the cause of the public distress; by recommending and facilitating a rising to plunder the public stores and magazines, and the property of the rich, whose affluence is the natural subject of envy to the poor.

It is, notwithstanding, to be observed that however defective may be the morality of the English people, they have still a respect for the laws and their magistrates, even in the moment of insurrection; it will be therefore advisable to spare, as much as possible, the property of those who may be in any civil function, and even of the country gentlemen; all impositions should be laid on the peers, the men of rank and high fortune, the clergy, those who serve as officers, in the army, navy, and especially in the militia, of all such, the country seats, farms, woods, cattle and corn should be given up to be plundered by the people: these predatory excursions should be made in different and even distant quarters by detachments of two or three hundred men each.

Extremities, such as these, rendered necessary by those of the Republic, and justified by the reflection that our cruel enemy has shewed the first example, will attract numbers of artizans and workmen, of vagabonds and idlers, and even of malefactors; but especial care must be taken not to incorporate them into the legion; they are to be formed into new companies, commanded by French officers, and to the end that the natives may not be acquainted with the force employed, these companies are to be kept asunder and in ignorance of the details as far as circumstances will permit; it is principally by these new formed companies that the insurrection is to be forwarded. The commerce of the enemy in the country is to be interrupted by breaking down bridges, cutting of dykes, and ruining causeways, which is, at the same time, essentially necessary for the preservation of the army; by plundering all convoys of subsistence, the public stages and waggons, and even private carriages; the cutting off of supplies of provisions from the principal towns, burning all vessels and boats in the rivers and canals, destroying magazines, setting fire to docks and coal yards, rope works, great manufactories, etc. etc. It is to be observed likewise, that by these means, a crowd of artizans will be thrown out of employment, and of course ready to embark in any measure which holds out to them subsistence and plunder without labour or fatigue.

The success of the expedition will likewise be materially forwarded by disarming the militia, by burning the arsenals in the seaports, by stopping the couriers of government, by seducing the enemy's troops to desert, and by the terror which the success of the legion and the progress of the insurrection will carry into the bosoms of the unwarlike citizens. The country most favourable for this system is that which is naturally strong, and in which there are forges and manufactures.

Subsistence is to be seized wherever it can be found; if any town or village refuse to supply it in the moment, it is to be given up to immediate pillage.

In order to spread panic as generally as possible, the legion is to be divided into several columns, having settled a common rendezvous, where they are to assemble every four, six, or eight days; the inhabitants must be obliged to serve as guides, and any who refuse are to be punished on the spot; the magistrates, or some of their families, are always to be employed in preference on this service, that they may not accuse or punish the others.

All denunciations against those who join the legion are to be punished by death. Wherever the legion or any of its columns is posted, if the neighbouring parishes do not give instant notice of the approach of the enemy, whether by ringing of bells, or otherwise, they are to be given up to fire and sword. For the safety of the troops under his command, Colonel Tate will avoid, as much as possible, all engagements with the regular forces, and will instead thereof, attack detachments, beat up their quarters, surprize their outposts etc. He will encourage all deserters and prisoners to enter into the new companies before mentioned; should such prisoners refuse, he will shave their heads and eyebrows, and if they are taken in arms they are to be shot.

Colonel Tate will not omit to observe, that there are in England numbers of French, who will be eager to join him, such as prisoners of war, soldiers and sailors, privates in the emigrant regiments, and a crowd of others, whom want and the desire of vengeance will draw to his standard; he may admit such Frenchmen into the legion; but he will observe to be on his guard that the newcomers may not raise cabals or factions; especially if there should be among them any nobles or priests, whose ambition is only to be exceeded by their cowardice; should any such attempt be made, he will take care to punish it most severely. Should the militia or volunteers of any district oppose the march of the legion, such district is to be severely punished, the militia or volunteers to be disarmed, their arms to be distributed among the insurgents, and all ammunition to be carefully preserved.

Finally, Colonel Tate will always remember to avail himself of the talents of the principal officers who surround him; he will profit of all favourable circumstances to acquire for his party the force and confidence necessary to ensure success; he will spare, and even sustain, the poor and the aged, the widow and the orphan, and will force the great, who are the cause of all our evils, to sustain the whole burden of the war.

(signed) Le Gen. Le Hoche.

After this lengthy set of instructions, Hoche added a few more details of a general nature for Tate's action in the field:

It would be imprudent to remain any length of time on the coast, after having effected your landing; you will doubtless see the necessity of penetrating into the country, and specially into the counties of Cheshire and Lancashire, not to speak of the opportunities which those counties afford you, by means of the mountains, to avoid the pursuit of the enemy, the field of your operations will be more extended: with boldness and intelligence combined, you may easily possess yourself of Chester or Liverpool, which you will ruin by burning the magazines, and filling up the ports, or at least you may cut off all communication between those cities and the interior. There is another object which should likewise decide you to enter those counties, as you will be joined there by two other columns of French troops, to which you will unite that under your command, if the general commanding the expedition in chief shall desire it.

It is therefore of consequence that you direct your march, from the very moment of landing, upon the town of Chester, where you will pass the Dee, beyond which you are to establish yourself.

Your march should be rapid and bold; you must not keep the main roads, but on the contrary proceed by byepaths and hollow ways, which are at a distance from the high road. Before you enter any village or town, you are to inform yourself whether there be any troops there, and what is their number; whether it be enclosed with walls and barriers, etc., and you are to take your measures in consequence.

You should frequently change your guides, and in order to mislead the enemy as to your destination, you should often make counter marches, and always mention to the guide you quit a road different from that which you mean to take, asking the way to the town or village on which you mean to turn your back, or at least whither you do not mean to go.

In order to spread the consternation and astonishment as wide as possible, after the destruction of Liverpool (for this point is capital) you must follow your blow, and seize upon some small town or seaport on that coast, which you will lay under contribution. You may be sure that immediately all the principal places will demand for their protection troops from the government, which is in want of them, and will of course be obliged to separate those of which it can dispose, by which means you will be able to destroy a great number by beating in detail the detachments which may be sent against you. The mobiliary columns can alone be successfully opposed to you, but even in that case it will be easy for you to destroy their effect. If they be weak, you will unite your forces and crush them; if they be strong, by scattering yourselves and committing hostilities in a hundred different quarters; the towns, which will be terrified by these means, will soon demand the troops which compose the columns to protect them from your parties, who will thereby remain masters of the field, and starve both the troops and the inhabitants. I doubt much whether the English know as yet the nature and use of mobiliary columns, but even if they do, you may find means to render them useless, because the government has not troops in number sufficient to guard all the points at once, and parties like yours may over-run the country in a thousand different directions.

Your soldiers are to carry with them nothing but their arms, ammunition, and bread: they will find everywhere clothes, linen and shoes; the inhabitants must supply your wants, and the seats of the gentry are to be your magazines.

In case the country, being exhausted, should offer you no further resources, or that a strong body of troops should force you to quit the place where you had established yourself, you are to depart with promptitude and expedition, make forced marches, and in the night, reposing yourself by day in the woods and mountains; if you are obliged to halt, in order to procure provisions you must first choose a strong position, from which you will send detachments into the neighbouring villages; it is with your cavalry (for you must take care from the first to mount a sufficient number of your troops) that you are to make this kind of excursion, you will also observe to re-mount your cavalry as often as necessity may require it.

Marching in this manner, unencumbered with baggage, your troops cannot be overtaken by the enemy; but if it should so happen that you are obliged to stand an engagement, you must remember that you are now a Frenchman, in as much as you command Frenchmen, and let that incite you to attempt a brilliant stroke; remember, however, that nothing but inevitable necessity should induce you to hazard the issue of a combat, and in that case you must supply by courage the defect of numbers. Should you be forced to clear your way through the enemy, you must commence the attack, but it must always be by night. About eleven o'clock, or midnight, send out two or three patrols of four or six men each, with orders to set fire to a dozen houses in your rear, in different quarters; the enemy, believing that you are running away, will most probably pursue you, in which case you may lay an ambuscade, or you may avoid him, or you may fall on the rear of one of his columns, which you may cut off with facility, in the dark and the confusion of an unexpected attack. If the enemy should run to extinguish the fires, you have the same advantages; you have your choice, either to avoid him, or which is still better, to beat him; if he remains under arms, and sends out patrols to reconnoitre, you must interrupt them, and put them to the bayonet, without firing a shot, and then, after two or three hours, you must form the column, and advance rapidly, *au pas de charge*, on one of his wings, which you will certainly rout, and then, without pushing the affair further, you will pursue your route, and remember to make in that day two or three countermarches.

In this manner you may, by a brilliant action, surprise in the night time and cut off a post which may be opposed to you in the daylight and open field you ought not, with the force under your command, to hesitate to attack two thousand of the enemy, and in the night, four or even five thousand; you ought to dislodge eight hundred from a post, not being intrenched; but if intrenched, and especially with cannon you are not to attack them.

In order to pass a river, where the bridges are guarded or broken down, if you cannot procure boats, you must endeavour to remount towards the source, in order to find a passage by means of a ford, a mill dam, etc. If you are hard pressed, you must strain a stout rope from one bank to the other, and pass your troops; those who do not know how to swim, holding fast by the rope, and carrying their firelocks slung over their shoulders, with the muzzle downwards to avoid wetting the lock; if trees can be found on the bank long enough to reach across, they are still better than ropes; in which case you will fell several of them. If the river, though fordable, be so deep as to take the soldiers up to their necks, you must make the best swimmers pass first, and the others follow by ranks, each soldier holding the next man strongly with the left hand by the skirt of the coat, and carrying his firelock in the right: by these means those who reach the opposite bank first will sustain the others, and assist them in getting out of the water: your horses will also be of use, but you must not reckon upon them.

In case your position should at last be no longer tenable, or that superior forces should force you to quit the country bordering on the Channel, you must not lose an instant to join the two French parties sent into the counties of York, Durham, and Northumberland. In that case you must send me notice into Ireland, that I may be enabled to execute a diversion in your favour. An officer in disguise may reach me, either by seizing a fishing boat on the coast of Wales, or else by route of Scotland.

I count upon your firmness and your courage; you may equally rely upon the gratitude of the French nation and my esteem and regard in particular.

My intention in giving you these instructions is less that you should attach yourself to the letter, than to the spirit of what they contain; and I leave to your judgment to make modification therein as circumstances may tender necessary.

(Signed) Le Gen. Le Hoche.

The most interesting aspect of Hoche's plan is that he does not appear to have considered that Tate's force should be anything other than the cream of the French army. Only in the penultimate paragraph does he speak of the possibility of 'superior forces' interfering and even then he holds out the possibility that Tate can meet up with Quantin's force which, in the event, did not even leave the English Channel. It is very strange that no redrafting was made in February after Hoche's return from Bantry Bay. By then the scheme had almost been forgotten and Hoche, somewhat in disgrace after the failure of the entire Irish invasion plan, had been posted to Commander-in-chief of the Army of Sambre et Meuse, a position often considered to be promotion when in fact it was a sideways move, or even a demotion, for the young General.

On 11 December, shortly before he left for Bantry Bay, General Hoche wrote to the Directory from Brest: 'I have entrusted to a man of brains and experience the command of the Second Legion of Francs, which I have raised here as secretly as possible. It is composed of 600 men drawn from all the prisons in my district, who are collected in two forts or islands, to prevent them escaping. To them I join 600 choice convicts from the galleys still in irons. They will be well armed and equipped.'

What sort of man was Hoche's 'Man of brains and experience'? William S. Tate was born about 1737 in Wexford, Ireland and went to America with his father, mother and two brothers, Robert and James, at an early age.[18] They settled near Charleston, South Carolina and shortly afterwards Tate's parents were killed in an Indian raid. The local Indians appeared to have been partisans of the British and this act helped to make Tate violently anti-British. However he worked with his brothers until the start of the War of Independence at the 26 Mile Creek ironworks, eight miles from Pendleton court house, outside Charleston. When war reached this area, South Carolina's governor, Lord William Campbell, forced to take shelter in a British ship in September 1775, wrote home to say that 'I most sincerely lament I cannot prevent the ruin I foresee.' It was time for the loyalists and republicans to divide and without hesitation William

Tate joined the newly formed republican artillery regiment as a Lieutenant at £1 15s. a day plus a bounty of £25 for every volunteer. He had seen the departure of Campbell before the action started but fate saw to it that another Campbell would cross his path. By 1779 Tate had become a Captain-Lieutenant in command of two pieces of artillery. He was particularly good at interrogating Indians and also served on a court martial board, probably because he was older than other officers of his rank. Getting enough money to live comfortably must have been a problem and Tate liked living in style. This may account for his action in 1780 when he was arrested on 8 March for making 'a false and improper return'. Major Mitchell took him to the Commanding Officer of the South Carolina Continental Artillery who ordered him to be reprimanded 'agreeable to the Sentence of the Court tomorrow morning at Roll Calling.'[19]

When Charleston surrendered to the British, Tate was made a prisoner. The experience did not improve his liking for his captors. However, he appears to have soon been exchanged for he served until the end of the war. By 1785 he was out of the army having collected a certificate of back pay from Commissioner Pierce for £1,919 'on interest from the 1st May 1783 being in full for balance of Pay and Commentation due me by the United States as Capt. Lt. of Artillery in this Line.'

He obtained 300 acres of land on the west bank of the Keowee river as an extra bounty and with some of his army colleagues formed the Carolina branch of the Society of Cincinnati for ex-officers. The Society still flourishes today.

In 1787 Tate married and 'seriously considering the uncertainty of life' wrote his will. He left one-third of his estate to his wife Elizabeth and two-thirds to his nephew William, son of his brother Samuel in Ireland, and on his wife's death the nephew was to inherit everything. It seems that Tate did not think his wife capable of looking after his interests and the marriage does not seem to have been a success.

With the help of Alexander Moultrie, a former Attorney General in Carolina, Tate formed the South Carolina Yazoo Company to exploit land on the Mississippi. Moultrie had access to public money and in 1792 he was impeached for fraudulently misusing £60,000 and the company collapsed.

Tate, not seriously affected by this, although he must have lost money, promptly launched himself headlong into a new adventure more suited to his capabilities. Genet, the new French Minister to the United States, landed in Charleston in 1793 and soon became an embarrassment to the government. French privateers began using American east coast ports and Genet planned a raid by American volunteers and French irregulars on Spanish Louisiana. Mangourit, French Consul in Charleston, looked for leaders and his eye fell on Tate, whom he described in a letter to Genet as having 'all the virtues of the adventurers who conquered the two Indies without their vices and ignorance; extremely severe to himself, drinking nothing but water; ... a firm disciplinarian and having in his brain the coolness and heat necessary to execute a great enterprise with small means. He conceives in the minute, decides on the instant, he carves in the right joint [i.e. does things the right way].'[20]

This report reached the Directory in France and no doubt Hoche read it with interest. A three-pronged force was planned to attack Florida led by Tate, Major Clarke of the Georgia Militia, and Samuel and Abner Hammond. By January 1794 Tate reported to Genet that he had collected 2,000 men, presumably on paper. Mangourit supplied the finance and William Moultrie, Governor of South Carolina and brother of the luckless Alexander added his official support. A 'D-day' of 10 April was set for a night attack on St. Augustine by six privateers. A rendezvous was established and all the marching routes worked out.

In Philadelphia, however, Secretary of State Jefferson had other ideas. He realised that a civil war could start if Genet was allowed to go ahead and he instructed Morris, U.S. Minister in Paris, to obtain Genet's recall.[21] It came in February, when his successor, Fauchet, arrived at Charleston. Genet was summoned to Paris, but fearing the worst, fled to New York where he married the daughter of Governor Clinton and retired from the political scene to a farm at Jamaica Village, Long Island. Alexander Hamilton, Treasury Secretary, commented 'the stormy petrel, his wings clipped, became a harmless and completely domesticated lovebird.'

Once more Tate was left in the lurch. He was threatened with arrest, for Colonel Wade Hampton was ordered to take Tate and two of his colleagues, John Hamilton and Stephen Drayton, into custody, but on Genet's dismissal nothing was done.[22] Tate had spent a considerable amount of his own money on the French cause and determined to get some of it back and, for he was an idealist rather than a mercenary, he crossed to France. He was thus one of the few Americans to believe that the French should be assisted by their fellow-revolutionaries in their struggle for freedom. One wonders whether he was really anxious to get out of Charleston, where things had gone wrong both with his career and his marriage. One suspects that he was restless and both considerations decided his action. He settled in the Hotel Boston in Paris, not far from Wolfe Tone's residence but the two did not meet as Tone writes later to Tate in terms of a stranger.[23]

In 1796 the Irish-American adventurer planned a privateer raid on Jamaica using Bermuda as a jumping-off point. He put the scheme before General Clarke at the Directory's war office. The General was a colleague of Tone's and co-planner with Hoche of the so nearly successful Irish expedition. Who could be more useful than Tate to Hoche and Clarke for a diversionary attack on the British mainland? Here was their man of 'brains and experience', a true revolutionary with an excellent reference from Mangourit. He spoke fluent English and his age might encourage the young French officers, who were to accompany him, to respect him.

The main target was Bristol, to be burnt by a landing party that should withdraw immediately. There was a strong possibility that it might succeed. Hoche did not know that Britain's second city was defended by the Marquis of Buckingham's militia, which was completely inexperienced and invincible only in the eyes of the Marquis. There were no naval ships patrolling the Bristol channel. For some strange reason the British government did not think the enemy could possibly reach Bristol and this myth lasted into the twentieth century, so that during the Second World War a German submarine succeeded in landing agents near Porlock with comparative ease. (The author's mother-in-law, then living at Oare, helped to capture one, who was dressed as a monk.)

4　Invasion

Gladsome day, we now remember
Thus the great event of old,
When our fathers were delivered
From the French invader bold.

Hardy local men and women,
Joined with Cawdor's noble name
Under heaven's kindly leading
Were the means to quench the flame.
Rev. J. Symonds, *Fishguard Centenary March*, 1897

Although Tone could well describe Tate's men as 'sad blackguards' who reminded him of the Dublin Green-boys (the prison thieves), they were equipped with the most modern French muskets and sailed in the most up-to-date ships in the French navy.

In command of the French naval force was Commodore J.J. Castagnier, an ex-Privateer captain who had distinguished himself at Dunkirk when he commanded the French gunboats that hampered the Duke of York's transports in 1792.

He was given two new ships, the frigates *Résistance* and the *Constance* and a two-year-old frigate, *Vengeance*, as a flagship, which had fought against Lord Bridport's squadron off the Ile de Groix on 22 June 1795, an indecisive action which did not enhance the reputation of the commander of the British channel fleet. The *Résistance*, built on the Loire, was armed with 28 18-pounders and 12 8-pounders. She weighed 1,182 tons and had a fair turn of speed. Her sister ship was the *Vengeance*. Most British frigates were only armed with 36 or 38 guns at this time and were smaller although their guns were usually 18-pounders and, on the whole, better managed. Thus, the *Indefatigable*, which had played a distinguished part in the Bantry Bay affair, was a 44-gun frigate which had been made out of a 64-gun ship of the line with one deck removed.[24] The *Constance* was a small 22-gun corvette of 520 tons with a new crew ably commanded by Captain Desauney, and to complete the squadron the lugger *Vautour*, 14 guns, was assigned to Castagnier. She was the first French ship home from Bantry Bay and was likewise to be the first ship home from Fishguard.

Tate's force of 600 regulars and 800 convicts was dressed in the English uniforms captured at Quiberon by Hoche in 1795. These had been died black. The men had long muskets and cutlasses and the officers were armed with simple swords, Tate's being no different from that of his non-commissioned officers. Many émigrés were included in the party; one such was the young Monsieur St. Amans, son of the Marquis de St. Amans, of whom we shall hear later. The second-in-command was Le Brun, the heir to the Baron de Rochemure, and there were three Irish officers two of whom, Captains Tyrrell and Morrison, Tate had probably known in America. The third, Lieutenant St. Leger, was to give an account of his part in the invasion which remains one of the main sources as to what occurred.

When the four ships left Brest for Camaret on 16 February, the troops were not told where they were going, their food supplies were limited and many were still in chains. Here, on *Vengeance* a mutinous legionnaire had to run the gauntlet of his fellow shipmates three times. On the 18th the wind was in the right quarter and the fleet sailed for Bristol.

There were no British ships in a position to spot them but when they neared the Cornish coast the following day they hoisted Russian colours. A small coaster coming too close in the dark was sunk by the *Vautour* and by midday on the 20th they were off Lundy, waiting for a change in the tide to get up to Bristol. Two small ships from Ilfracombe were captured and sunk. Their crews were imprisoned and as the wind freshened the little fleet sailed up to Porlock with difficulty when Castagnier suggested to Tate that they should cross over and land at Swansea. Tate consulted his orders, but after an argument became convinced that they could not reach Bristol before daylight so he agreed to be dropped at Cardigan Bay rather than Swansea, which was deemed too close to British ships, Castagnier obtained a pilot to guide him up the Welsh coast in one of the prisoners from the Ilfracombe ships.

Meanwhile in Ilfracombe itself the two small coasters had been missed and lookouts had reported the strange ships off Lundy. On Lantern Hill at Ilfracombe Betsy Gammon, a local fishwife and member of the local

Militia as so many men were at sea, beat her drum and the British Sea Fencibles were called out.[25] At Bideford Lt. Col. Orchard addressed the North Devon Volunteers, who hurriedly assembled when they heard the news from Ilfracombe. 'In four hours' reported the Colonel, 'I found every officer and man that was ordered on parade at Bideford ready and willing to march ... silent, orderly and sober as might be expected at a morning parade of an old regiment ... As I was preparing to march I received an account that the French ships were gone from the coast and that Tranquility had restored again to the town [Ilfracombe].'[26]

On the 22nd Samuel Hancorne, Customs Collector of Swansea, wrote to the Home Secretary, the Duke of Portland, with the news that a St. Ives ship had spotted four foreign ships near Lundy between 10a.m. and 4p.m. the previous day. Another St. Ives ship, the *Dolphin*, had signalled to them but had not received a reply. The Regulating Captain of Swansea port promptly sent messages to his counterparts at Plymouth, Milford Haven and Bristol (these men were in charge of naval stores and the victualling of visiting naval ships) and a copy to the Admiralty with the clear news that in his opinion these were enemy ships, Russian flags or no Russian flags.

By now Castagnier had reached St. Davids where he was spotted at about 10a.m. on the 22nd by Mr. Williams of Trelethin, an old sailor. His wife, whose eyesight was better, took the telescope and noted English flags. As a traditional verse has it:

> Mr. Williams Trelethin did know every tide
> From England to Greenland without guide
> Mrs. Williams Trelethin did take the spye-glass
> And then she cried out-There they was.

Mrs. Williams had helped to rescue some wrecked Swedish sailors on the Bishop rocks a few years before and the couple were well known as a result. Even with so many captured ships in use by the British navy, Williams, an ex-sailor, was sure they were French, probably because they were close in shore and not following the normal route. It is unlikely that Tate would have allowed the soldiers on deck, as their black uniforms would have only increased any onlooker's suspicion.

A servant went galloping off to St. Davids to warn the inhabitants. At Solva a few miles away Mr. Whitesides, a Liverpool engineer who had

The fort on Castle Point overlooking Fishguard harbour which fired a shot at the
Vautour

recently erected the Smalls Lighthouse, collected a body of seamen together, some of whom were armed with muskets, their number including two tall lads equipped only with straight scythes. Whitesides placed himself on a horse he had hired from a Mr. Barzey and took command.[27]

At 2p.m. the ships anchored off Fishguard and the *Vautour* went round Pen Anglas to examine the harbour. Still flying British colours she was greeted by a shot from the fort. This remarkably prompt action has often been ascribed to the fort having received a signal, but it seems more likely that Williams's messenger had reached Fishguard and had gone straight to the fort where Ensign Bowen of the Fencibles was on duty with three gunners, who were then prepared for the enemy ships. Alarmed, the *Vautour* beat a hasty retreat.

Meanwhile a small sloop, the *Britannia*, carrying a cargo of culm for Colonel Knox tried to get into Fishguard. The *Vengeance* sent a shot across her bows and removed her master, John Owen, and his crew in a ship's boat. Owen was taken to see Castagnier and on the way bumped into a fellow Welshman, James Bowen. The latter had been a servant at Trehowel farm on Pencaer but had been dismissed by his master, Mr.

Carregwastad Point, where the French troops disembarked

Mortimer, and transported for horsestealing. It is possible that the ship he had left on had been captured by a French ship that had taken him to Brest where Tate had enrolled him as a guide. This would account for the fleet anchoring off Carregwastad Point, and later using Mortimer's house as a headquarters.

Owen was taken to Castagnier's cabin where he met 'a very fine looking man who spoke good English.' On interrogation he was asked how many defenders there were in Fishguard. Quickly counting the Fencibles he doubled their number and added a few more saying 500, all well armed. This was in fact nearly correct as events turned out but Owen could not have known. Tate and Castagnier had a hurried consultation and decided to land the troops. The ship's boats were launched about 5p.m. on a night remarkably calm and mild.

Lieutenant St. Leger and the grenadiers were the first ashore.[28] They had to scramble up a steep cliff rising to 200ft. but well provided with clefts and gullies in which one man could follow another. It must have been a clear night for the men had no trouble getting ashore, although one boat, which may well have carried a four-pounder cannon, capsized with some ammunition. A sponson (a sponge on a stick used for cleaning out cannon barrels) was later washed ashore and a French cannon stands outside one of the Pencaer farmhouses today. It may well have been recovered from the sea, but there is no record of Tate, a former gunner, bringing artillery — this was against his orders and would have hindered his march to Chester.

French cannon now at Trenewydd

From a list made after their surrender, it is known that in a remarkably short space of time 47 barrels of gunpowder, ten hampers of equipment, a sheet of ball cartridge, 12 boxes of handgrenades and most of the 1,400 men and two women (wives of soldiers who came as laundry maids) reached the top of the cliff. St. Leger and the Irish officers made for Trehowel farm, no doubt guided by Bowen, where they broke open the door and found a feast prepared and the signs of a hurried departure. Mr. Mortimer, thinking the ships were British, had ordered his servants to prepare a meal for the officers. He just had time to look again and see the French flags before the boats set out for the shore. Saddling his horse he left for Llanwnwr, a nearby farmhouse, whilst, according to local tradition, his servant Annie George collected all the silver spoons and walked to Llanwnwr with a fellow servant who was carrying a mug of *cwrwdda*, the local beer. In spite of the oncoming French not a drop was spilt.[29]

Tate came ashore and, probably at Bowen's suggestion, made his headquarters at Trehowel. The majority of the troops camped at the top of the cliff in the vicinity of the present monument. Camp fires were lit of gorse and shrub and sentries were posted at vantage points, St. Leger being given command of a party of grenadiers that occupied Carnwnda rocks, the site of an early fort, and a natural defensive point. The troops who had not got ashore slept in comfort in the anchored frigates. Most of the men were hungry and short work was made of the Trehowel geese, ducks and other livestock. The occupation had so far been a resounding success. The supplies were landed, the ships remained in case of sudden attack from the sea and by good fortune or by Bowen's careful navigation their position on Pencaer was such that it would be extremely hazardous for the British to attack. French troops stood on the commanding height of Carnwnda and with an early start the port of Fishguard, a stepping stone for Hoche to bring fresh reinforcements, could be theirs for the asking. The secret to success would have been a rapid communication with Brest and a follow-up expedition. Fortunately for Fishguard radio sets had not been invented and the Directory were not sufficiently intuitive to send more ships, they were more interested in rescuing the four ships that had left Brest. They did not worry about Tate's men, in fact it was a relief to get rid of them.

Castagnier remained off Carragwasted until the afternoon of 23 February. He then summoned a conference on *Vengeance* attended by his captains, Tate and a few of his other officers. A code of flag signals was arranged should he return and Tate was rowed ashore, upon which Castagnier proceeded as instructed to Dublin roads. The original plan had been to prevent British reinforcements landing there assuming the Bantry Bay expedition had succeeded and there had been an army of 15,000 Frenchmen at loose in Ireland. Hoche's original plans had not been altered although the Bantry Bay expedition had returned to Brest.

Castagnier's ships were fortunate in overrunning a fleet of nearly 12 small transports carrying Irish recruits for the British army on the way, which they sank and captured 400 prisoners. Heading out towards the

Trehowel farm in the 1970s

Scillies to avoid any escorts looking for this convoy, Castagnier decided once more to head for Ireland having despatched the *Vautour* to Brest with a message for Admiral Morard de Galles. Off Cape Clear the weather worsened and *Vengeance* lost her main yard, which was not fatal, but *Résistance* lost her rudder and had to be towed by *Constance*.

Meanwhile the Admiralty, warned by Captain Longcroft, the Regulating Captain for Haverfordwest, and later by Admiral Kingsmill in Cork, had sent three Plymouth-based ships (the *Shannon*, commanded by Captain Fraser with the *Beaulieu* and *Mercury*) to patrol Lundy Island. The *Shannon* had 46 guns and the others 36 and 40 respectively. Lord Bridport's Spithead fleet also put to sea and Sir Harry Burrard Neale in *St. Fiorenzo* (36 guns) was cruising between the Isle of Wight and the French coast. On 3 March Sir Harry joined the British fleet blockading Bordeaux and on 8 March he met up with *La Nymphe*, another 36-gun British frigate, off Ushant. These two vessels caught up with the *Constance* and *Résistance* off Brest. The storm damaged *Résistance* was in tow from *Constance*. The action that followed is best described in the crisp words of the log of the *St. Fiorenzo*:

> Standing in for Brest Water at 5, found the Main Top Mast sprung and stood out. Am employed getting up new Main Top Mast, wore and stood towards Brest. Observed 14 sail of the line and 6 frigates in Inner Road. K [possibly the officer of the watch] saw 2 sail in the Offing, which proved to be two frigates. Bore down and prepared for action. 50 minutes past the big ship struck, at 10 the small one struck. Pt. St. Matthews NNE 4 miles, getting the prisoners on board.

The danger to *Résistance*'s rudder had been her undoing. She was in no state to fight but the little *Constance* lost her main mast and fore-top mast in the action. On board *Résistance* ten men were killed and nine wounded. On *Constance* eight men were killed and six wounded. Both ships were taken in tow and, despite the weather, arrived safely in Plymouth.

Sir Harry wrote a report to Lord Bridport on the action praising by name 'Lieutenants Durell, Farnall and Renwick of *St. Fiorenzo* and Lieutenants Irvine, Lawrence and Masters of *La Nymphe*.' The marine officers were also mentioned, especially Lieutenant Campbell of *La Nymphe* and her captain John Cooke. A special medal was cut for the action.

The Capture of The Résistance and The Constance as painted by Nicholas Pocock (courtesy of the National Maritime Museum)

Sir Harry was pleased with his prizes:

> *La Résistance* commanded by Monsieur Montagne, mounting 48 guns, eighteen pounders on her main deck and manned with 345 men: she is only six months old, built upon a new construction and is in every respect one of the finest Frigates the French had and certainly the largest, measuring 45ft beam. The other Frigate is *La Constance* commanded by Monsr. Desauney mounting 24 Nine pounders upon the main deck and manned with 189 men; she is two years old and a very fine ship. These are two of the Frigates which landed the troops in Wales, it is a pleasing circumstance to have completed the failure of that expedition.

The *Vautour* and the *Vengeance* arrived home safely but the latter was captured in Jamaican waters in 1800 by the *Seine* and added to the British fleet, although she was never again fit to sail.

The *Résistance* was repaired and renamed *Fisgard* (spelling the port in the old way) and in 1798 she had a famous battle with the frigate *L'Immortalité* in which the French General Ménago, hero of Quiberon, was killed. Later, with her famous commander Captain Byam Martin, she attacked Corunna and was present at Curaçao and the Earl of Chatham's Walcheren expedition. The *Constance* was wrecked off Brittany in 1806 and recaptured by the French who repaired her in St. Malo.

5   The Battle that didn't take place

Tate, safe behind Llanwnda rocks,
Was not afraid of Colonel Knox;
Knox, safe behind the turnpike gate,
Was not afraid of Colonel Tate
Traditional verse

For many years after the event and even today the night of 22 February has been traditionally fine in Pembrokeshire with a calm sea. 'All nature, earth and ocean were at peace' wrote one observer afterwards.[30] At Tregwynt, a large farmhouse sheltering in a wooded valley a few miles from Carregwastad Point, there was a ball for the younger militia officers, including Thomas Knox. Mrs. Harries, the elderly widow of Captain George Harries, had one of the finest ballroom floors in Pembrokeshire with an elaborate system of springs. It was on the first floor and as the guests were sitting down to dinner on the ground floor there was a loud knocking at the front door.

One of the Fencibles stood there trembling. 'Come quickly,' he said addressing Knox, who may have recognised the man in the light of the oil lamp, 'the French are landing at Pencaer.'[31] There was complete panic. Knox picked up his cloak and dashed out to find his horse. Mrs. Harries and her family went round collecting all their valuables, some of which were hidden in the house and have never been found to this day.[32] The coach was brought round to the door by the servants and George and Thomas Harries put their mother and her hastily assembled luggage on board and set out for a friend's house at Narberth. The food stood uneaten and the lights burnt. One man remained; because of his age and 'informities' as Knox described them, Daniel Vaughan, brother of Gwynne, the fort's commander, went round the house loading all available firearms and bolting the doors.

Proceeding to Fishguard by the coast track, Knox was very curious about the messenger's report.[33] Why should the French land at Pencaer? Fishguard or Goodwick perhaps, but to risk the cliffs at night in winter was most unlikely. He saw the four ships as he trotted past and stopped to look at them. He thought they must be English frigates escorting Dutch East Indiamen. At Fishguard fort he found Ensign Bowen and 70 Fencibles waiting for him. An unknown volunteer appeared who introduced himself as Thomas Nesbitt. He was a half-pay officer waiting for transhipment to Ireland and he was to be a tower of common sense and strength to Knox in the next few days. Like Vaughan he was one of the few to keep his nerve and, because of Knox's hesitation and uncertain information, he offered to take charge of the team of scouts which were sent out in all directions. The offer was readily accepted.

Knox heard about the fort's moment of glory when they had fired at the *Vautour* and decided that they must fire again as a signal for Major Bowen's contingent at Llwyngwair on the Cardigan road. He also sent a messenger to the Major to ask him to bring as much ball cartridge as he could find from the store at Dinas. He finished his letter by saying that if he found it necessary he would retreat towards Newport, which was where Bowen was coming from and could mean that the two groups would meet on the road.

At 8.20p.m. William Williams, a local man, came proudly into the fort and showed Knox a wound he said he had received from a French bullet. He had been captured by 12 men in strange uniforms, he said, and when he escaped in the dark they had fired at him. Sergeant Roberts was sent out to the spot where Williams had been attacked and a further message

Llwyngwair, home of Major Bowen, photographed in the early 1970s

Lord John Cawdor (1755-1821) by Sir Joshua Reynolds (courtesy of Cawdor Castle)

was sent to Bowen. Knox seemed to enjoy using his pen for he also had time to write to Lord Milford, Colonel of the Pembroke Yeomanry and Lord Lieutenant of the county.

Stricken with gout, Lord Milford was woken up at about 10.30p.m. by a horseman clattering into his castle yard at Picton. The heavy bolt was drawn back and Lewis Mathias, father of one of his lordship's servants, was ushered into the bedroom. Three letters were handed over, a brief one from Knox saying 'we are in confusion but endeavouring everything for the best' and two of the original warning notes, one from Williams of Trelethin and the other from a Mr. Tucker of Sealyham. In spite of his incapacity, Milford acted with speed. He sent a messenger to Lord Cawdor and at 2a.m. wrote to Knox saying he had ordered the Cardigan Militia, Captain Ackland's corps and Lord Cawdor's troop to get to Fishguard as soon as possible.

In Haverfordwest an earlier messenger had stopped to give Colonel Colby the news and a committee was soon formed of prominent people, amongst whom was Colby's second-in-command, Captain Scourfield of Robeston. Captain Longcroft was also a member and had sent out a summons to his sailors in Milford Haven. There were two cutters, *Diligence* and *Speedwell* in the harbour and their crews set about landing their 9lb. cannon, four per cutter, and dragging them to Haverfordwest. It must have been about midnight when Lord Cawdor was woken from his peaceful slumber by Lord Milford's messenger. He fortunately did not have to summon his men as they were already due to parade early next morning for a funeral in Haverfordwest.

The Committee meeting broke up at about 9p.m. and Colonel Colby and the Hon. Captain Edwardes, who was later appointed ADC to Lord Cawdor, set out to Fishguard to reconnoitre, probably fearful that young Knox would not be able to cope with the situation. They found Knox almost alone in the fort, the Fencibles having been despatched on errands and on scouting parties. It was very dark but Colby ascertained Knox's positions, advising him, as Knox stated later, to retreat. Edwardes and Colby made their way back to Haverfordwest to report to their Committee.

Meanwhile two French stragglers had been picked up and one, who spoke English or possibly Irish, said that the French numbered between 1,200 and 1,400 men. When Knox received the news he thought the man was lying and at sunrise he gave the order to retreat, although by then he had been reinforced by Major Bowen's men. The invalid gunners in the

40

Manorowen in the 1970s; the summer house in the garden was attacked by the French

fort were ordered to spike their guns and throw the ammunition over the cliff. A local shopkeeper, Mr. Davies, who had supplied most of the ammunition was horrified. He spoke to Nesbitt and with the help of the three gunners the ammunition was brought out in a cart and the guns left unspiked. Ensign Bowen, no relation of the Major, led the rearguard and had Tate's men been waiting, Fishguard could have been occupied without force.

At about 10a.m. the Fencibles halted for bread and cheese and, marching in a broken line, they reached Trefgarne en route for Haverfordwest when the Haverfordwest contingent came into view. Lord Cawdor, placed in overall command by the Committee, had soon got under way and in spite of a letter from Lord Milford suggesting Colby should take command, had by his presence been universally accepted as leader. Knox disputed this as Lord Cawdor was only a Captain and he, Knox, was a Colonel. The two men had a few hasty words — it is apparent that later they planned a duel — and the Fencibles took up a position in the rear of the column.

At 5p.m. the party reached Manorowen house and the first action occurred. A party of French were seen making for the summer house and Lord Cawdor sent a few horsemen over to occupy it. Shots were fired but the French escaped in the dark to warn Tate.

Lord Cawdor could now take stock of his force. It was a real Gilbert and Sullivan army with a strange mixture of uniforms, but considering the little time in which it had been gathered, it was remarkably large for an area in which there were no barracks, no large towns and only volunteers to rely on, together with the navy. It consisted of:

	Officers	Men
Lord Cawdor's Yeomanry Cavalry		
	Major Ackland	
	Major Lloyd	
	Act. Cornet. Adams	43
Cardigan Militia		
	Lieut. and Adjt. Cole	
	Lieut. Davies	
	Ensign Price	100
Capt. Ackland's Pembroke Volunteers		
	Capt. Ackland	
	Lieut. Lort	
	Ensign Ridgway	93
Fishguard Fencibles		
	Lt. Col. Knox	
	Major Bowen	
	Ensign Bowen	191
Naval Party		
	Capt. Longcroft	
	Lieut. Dobbins	
	Lieut. Hopkins	
	Lieut. Meares	
	Lieut. Perkins	148
Oddments		
	Lord Cawdor	
Second-in-command	Colonel Colby	
ADCs	Capt. Davies of Coombe	
	John and Owen Phillips	
	Hon. Capt. Edwardes	
	Mr. Nesbitt	24
	Total	594

This 'army' was martialled at Manorowen into a fighting force with the Yeomanry in front and the naval party and their eight 9lb. cannon in carts in the rear.

Cawdor decided to approach Pencaer by a narrow lane leading up to the village of Llanwnda, then in French hands, and the next four hours are vividly described by Mr. Mansell, a gentleman volunteer from Bristol who was in the leading files. 'We found the enemy on a high mountain [Carnwnda] but couldn't ascertain their numbers,' he explained in a letter home, 'we marched up a very long and narrow road or lane, the banks on each side being very high and I believe the distance about ¾ of a mile. At about 8 o'clock at night we thought it most prudent to retreat ... there were 200 of them lying flat on their bellies. They wished us to begin the action as by that means they could see us. Their clothing was a very dark colour, next to black. Next morning we showed ourselves to the best advantage ... I am much fatigued, not having been to bed for three nights [having spent two days and nights travelling from Bristol] or closed my eyes.'[34] It was an experience for part-time soldiers, for having marched 17 miles from Haverfordwest, they were mad to climb the steep path in the dark to the unknown French positions. It must have been good scouting that discovered the ambush of 200 men, for there is no record of any shots being fired.

Lord Cawdor's men retired wearily to spend the night in Goodwick and Fishguard, most in the open and only the fortunate cramming into the tiny Royal Oak. Sentries were posted and an uneasy night passed.

There were other visitors to the scene of the Pencaer landing. A reverend gentleman descended the cliff and removed a finger from the Frenchman who had been thrown over and buried in a shallow grave. Gradually the man's skeleton was removed bone by bone for keepsakes. The Frenchman killed by the sailors of Solva had his ears cut off and one of them was kept by a peasant who met Major Bowling's servant shortly afterwards. Proudly showing his souvenir the peasant said he was going to show it to his family and to his neighbours. One little boy at Fishguard was presented with some cannon balls, 'a strange gift for a three year old' and sat on a Frenchman's knee playing with them. Another cannon ball was dug up quite recently near Pont Jago[35] and its calibre matches the 4lb. cannon that stands outside Trenewydd today, which could well have been the only one hauled up the beach. However, it is possible this was not a French cannon at all.

Tate's first action on daybreak, being unaware that Knox's actions had led to the temporary evacuation of Fishguard, was to attempt to find transport. Ever mindful of his instructions, he wanted to get off before the British fleet arrived. He sent out foraging parties in all directions and hoisted the tricolour on Carnwnda, the iron-age fort and his look-out point above Llanwnda. His men were hungry and what few animals remained in the area were slaughtered for food. Fortunately for Lord Cawdor, however, in January a Portuguese coaster had been wrecked nearby and there was hardly a farmhouse without a supply of Portuguese wine. Men soon became drunk as farms were looted and the officers found it difficult to control them.

Lieutenant St. Leger and 200 men were given the job of patrolling the approach to Fishguard and they were the men who lay down, muskets at the ready, when Lord Cawdor's troops approached with drums beating in the dark.

The French made no effort to hide their movements and one officer was observed walking along a field waving a flag in a futile attempt to rally men to his cause.

Small actions took place throughout the day, but there was no battle. Tate had never intended to fight one and his men were soon in no condition to call themselves soldiers. In one episode at Carngowil farm, a party of Frenchmen ran into a man on a horse with four others, all armed with sporting guns. This was Mr. Whitesides, the Liverpool lighthouse engineer, and a party of Solva men. 'Take care my boys and do it well,' he said to his men, 'faith I am afraid they will kill Mr. Barzey's horse.'[36] The muskets cracked and three Frenchmen fell, one never to rise again. One Welshman was wounded in the leg but was helped on to Mr. Barzey's horse. Later the Frenchman was buried where he was killed and the field today is called Parc-y-Francwr.

Elsewhere a Welsh farmer met a drunken Frenchman in a field and they had a fight. The Welshman finally killed his opponent with an ancient musket and then ran down to tell the nearest Militia officer: 'If you want to see a dead Frenchman, there is one in yonder field.'

A Welsh woman found a drunken soldier drinking at a well and coming up behind him pulled up his legs so he fell head down into the shaft. He survived to tell the tale.

At Brestgarn a Frenchman, hearing a click as if a musket was being loaded, fired blindly and hit a grandfather clock.

Mary Williams at Carlem ran out of her house when the French appeared and was wounded in the leg and raped. She lived on a fat government pension until she was 89 so by the time she died she had gained £2,240 from the incident.

At Cotts farm a woman had just been delivered of a child and the French quietly moved out of the farm once they had removed the available stock of wine.

Two Welshmen were shot and killed when they tried to protect their livestock. At another farm a peasant gave a soldier his food and while it was being eaten, crept up and walloped him with a chair leg. The soldier was asked later what had happened to him and replied that he had been given a light blow on the head.

At St. David's a blacksmith pronounced 'Here is a hatchet and there is the cathedral, it is better to have that than have the whole place burnt,' pointing to the lead on the roof. Men stripped some of it before the Dean could stop them. It was melted and turned into bullets; years later a bag was found at Martell Farm full of these bullets with a note stating that they were intended for use against the French invaders.

However the great Fishguard heroine of the day was a cobbler named Jemima Nicholas who was well able to hold her own with any man. She marched out with a pitchfork and captured 12 Frenchmen near Llanwnda. She then went back for more. She died in 1832 aged 82, her tombstone standing at the front of Fishguard church. She was outlived by another Fishguard lady, Nelly Phillips who lived to the age of 103 and in 1891 was able to talk about seeing the French ships sail round Strumble Head when she had been a nine-year-old cowgirl.[37]

Lord Cawdor also had support from the next door county. John Vaughan, Lord Lieutenant of Carmarthenshire, had been staying with Lord Cawdor and was on his way back to Golden Grove on

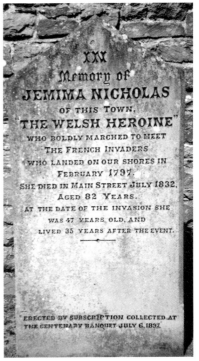

Monument to Jemima Nicholas

45

the afternoon of 22 February.[38] He had an express letter from the Mayor of Carmarthen the following day saying that '500 Frenchmen' had landed at Fishguard. He wrote to Lord Cawdor for details, saying 'I have long thought them mad but till now never considered them to be such fools as to choose so miserable a spot.' Thinking it must be privateers stealing cattle and sheep, he thought little more about it until a messenger rapped on his door at 2a.m. on the Friday morning. He rushed downstairs to find a letter from Lord Milford asking for help. He immediately took horse for Carmarthen ordering the Yeomen Cavalry to turn out and asked the Sheriff and Adjutant of Militia to get as many arms as possible for volunteers. He later wrote to Lord Cawdor saying what he had done:

> Very much to the credit of all ranks [of the Carmarthen Yeomanry] they turned out in a very handsome manner to a considerable number and I have no doubt had we such a number of arms, 5000 wou'd have appeared in a short time. They went as far as St. Clears on their way to Haverford West. On the road they received an Express saying that there was no Occasion for their proceeding. I came here with the intention of accompanying the March. I shall return immediately in case any Letters may be sent by Government to the Lieutenancy respecting the arrival of troops and their destinations, which I find have been applied for ... When you are at leisure pray send me a full Account of this expedition, which I conclude only appear with the intention of plundering the country.

In Towyn the local militia led by Captain Cresswell marched south and had covered several miles before they heard of the surrender.

6   The Surrender and Trials

'Thus ended the great fiasco of the French invasion.
What did it all mean?"
Edward Laws, *The History of Little England Beyond Wales*

Much has been written about the part played by the Welsh women in the Fishguard affair. John Mends of Haverfordwest wrote to his son in Essex about '400 women with red flannel over their shoulders, which the French at a distance took for soldiers, as they appeared all red.' He supported the argument that Lord Cawdor deliberately made the Welsh women in their stove-pipe hats and red whittles walk round a rock so that from a distance Tate would think they were the Guards. John and Mary Mathias wrote from Narberth on 27 February to their sister with the news that 'near four hundred women in Red flanes and Squier Cambel went to ask them were they to fight and they said they were and when they come near the French put down thair arms and they was all tok presoners that time and are brought to Haverfordwest Friday night last-not one kild but too of our men and five of the French by been to bould ...'.[39]

A more reliable source, Principal Salmon, states that the French had already surrendered by the time the women had arrived on the scene and it was only the locals like Jemima who actually went out and brought them in.[40] The arrival of Lord Cawdor on Thursday with his men coincided with the dusk and the colours of the British troops would be hard to distinguish. Lord Cawdor may well have asked the women if they had come to fight on Friday morning and been told yes. The women would have seen the approaching French not realising that by this time they were surrendering.

What induced Tate to surrender when events were going well for him? We must go back to Thursday afternoon when Tate and Castagnier held a hurried conference on board the *Vengeance*. A document was drawn up signed by 24 army and naval officers stating that Castagnier had done his duty and signals were arranged for the departure of the ships. Tate and the army officers were rowed ashore and shortly afterwards on receiving the signal from Tate the fleet withdrew. To stay any longer would have endangered the ships and Castagnier's orders were to make for Dublin roads then home to Brest.

The French were naturally disappointed in losing their ships so quickly. All must have thought of them as a link with home and it seems that apart from Tate and his more trusted officers their sailing off was a complete surprise. A conference was held at Trehowel farm in which stormy scenes took place — some of the more intoxicated officers threatened Tate with their muskets unless he surrendered.[41] The quartermaster reported that no carts were to be had and that provisions were low. Despite the fact that the brandy had been poured away to prevent further cases of drunkenness, without too much reluctance, Tate wrote to the 'Officer commanding His Britannick Majesty's Troops' in the following manner

> The Circumstances under which the Body of the French Troops under my command were landed at this Place renders it unnecessary to attempt any military operations, as they would tend only to Bloodshed and Pillage. The Officers of the whole Corps

The Royal Oak in Fishguard, that became the headquarters of the British staff

have therefore intimated their desire of entering into a Negociation upon Principles of Humanity for a surrender. If you are influenced by similar Considerations you may signify the same by the Bearer, and in the mean time, Hostilities shall cease.

> Health and Respect,
>> Tate
>>> Chef de Brigade [42]

L'Hanhard and Le Brun were sent to Fishguard with this letter at about 8 o'clock. It is a long walk, although downhill, but at Caerlem they met Thomas Williams who escorted them to the Royal Oak in Fishguard, which was then a private inn owned by Hugh Meyler. The officers assembled in the house heard Tate's letter read to them by Lord Cawdor who then passed it round to Colonel Colby, Major Ackland, the two Vaughans (Daniel had at last arrived from Tregwynt) and Colonel James of the Cardigan Militia. Knox was also present and blurted out that the French had 20,000 men, 10,000 of whom were in Fishguard.[43] Lord Cawdor, annoyed by the word 'Negotiation' said that they were only interested in an unconditional surrender and he sat down to write the following reply

> To the Officer Commanding the French Troops
> Sir,
> The Superiority of the Force under my Command, which is hourly increasing, must prevent my treating upon any Terms short of your surrendering your whole Force Prisoners of War.
> I enter fully into your wish of preventing an unnecessary effusion of Blood, which your speedy Surrender can alone prevent, and which will entitle you to that Consideration it is ever the Wish of British Troops to show an enemy whose numbers are inferior.
> My Major will deliver you this letter and I shall expect your Determination by Ten o'clock, by your Officer, whom I have furnished with an Escort, that will conduct him to me without Molestation.
>> I am etc., Cawdor[44]

Major Ackland and some of his troop escorted the French messengers back to Tate. The latter received Cawdor's letter in silence and early on Friday morning he wrote another letter stating:

The idea of the officers of the French corps is the same which you have expressed in your letter.

I therefore authorise Lt. Colonel Le Brun and Lieut. Faucon my ADC to meet such officers as you will appoint, to treat in the subject of the surrender of the troops in the usual form.

Salut et respect Tate[45]

Faucon arrived at the Royal Oak shortly afterwards and, according to tradition, the terms were signed on the small table that still stands in the bar. Lord Cawdor and his staff went to Henner Cross and on the climb up the steep hill they spotted a Frenchman fighting a Welsh peasant. Cawdor leapt off his horse to intervene.[46]

Tate probably signed the agreement later at Trehowel, but it has never subsequently come to light. Meanwhile Colonel Colby arranged his troops

The surrender of the French at Goodwick Sands, from a painting at Carmarthen Museum. The scene was painted somewhat crudely by a local artist and shows the militia on the hill with the three columns of French having placed their muskets on the sand. Lord Cawdor is on a white horse and the 20-odd horsemen of the Castlemartin Yeomanry cavalry are mostly in the foreground. Two ships are on the horizon indicating that the surrender was probably never seen by the artist, who has added, for good measure, a deserter being caught by three fierce Welsh women in the foreground

on the hills above Goodwick Sands. The hills were crowded with sightseers and as there was no sign of the French by midday, Cawdor sent his ADC, the Hon. Captain Edwards, to Trehowel accompanied by two horsemen and Mr. Millingchamp, the brother of Archdeacon Millingchamp of Llangoedmore, who carried a white flag.

The ADC's party found most of the French troops lined up ready to march. Tate gave the order to open pans and shed priming then the first column set off, its drummers beating the step. The invasion force, less some 25 sick and the few deserters, marched down the narrow lane to Goodwick where they stacked their muskets on the sand. Up at Trehowel, Tate remained with the sick being cared for by Surgeon Major Larand. Most of them were suffering from the effects of eating uncooked poultry and drinking the Portuguese wine.

John Mortimer, the young owner of Trehowel, chose this moment to return home. His house had been ransacked but the roof and some of the windows were intact. He was approaching the door when, as he subsequently described him, a lost looking old man in shabby clothes came up to him.

'Are you master here?', said Tate, 'I was so once.' Mortimer talked to him and asked why he had surrendered. 'I have often been in battle,' explained the American, 'over my shoes in blood but I have never felt such a sensation as when I first put my foot on British ground. My heart failed in a way I cannot describe.'[47] Tate handed his sword to Mortimer (his descendants still possess it) and some reports say left him the cannon, which had been brought ashore by the naval party. It was never used and would have been too cumbersome to transport without a heavy cart.

The prisoners were marched to Haverfordwest where most of them were shut up in the castle gaol. The remainder were locked in the three churches of St. Martin, St. Thomas and St. Mary. The fifers and drummers of the Yeomanry played the tune *By the girl I left behind me* which is

Tate's sword, now in private hands

Muskets taken from the French prisoners, on display in Cawdor Castle, Nairn, Scotland (courtesy of Cawdor Castle)

now known as *Lord Cawdor's March*, and en route Mortimer's servant Annie George recognised Bowen, who had once been a servant at Trehowel. A man from Llanwnwr was recognised by a blacksmith from Newbridge, but for the majority it was their first visit to Britain.

On 27 February the Duke of Portland wrote to Lord Milford asking him to report on the damage done by the French[48] and on the number of dead. Lord Milford replied at once saying this was being undertaken and 'As everything was now quiet' he wanted to take 'a survey tomorrow of the Sea Coast and to pitch upon Proper Places for Beacons.' There was a lot to do. Two men, George Bowen and Griffiths were despatched to round up stragglers and search for missing arms. They were surprised by not finding any bayonets and came to the conclusion that the French prisoners still retained them and that their knapsacks should be searched.[49] They were found and placed in carts with the muskets. (A ring bayonet is still on the musket that hangs in the Royal Oak.) Mr. Mathias, an alderman and magistrate of Haverfordwest, was given the job of working out the damage done by the French to private property. He wrote a long report to Lord Milford on his findings in which he said that he and Mr. Jordan examined the sufferers and they were assisted by Mr. Tucker of Sealyham, one of the original alarm raisers of the landing, and others so that people did not produce too many 'ridiculous and absurd charges.'

The worst damage was done at Trehowel and John Mortimer, described as 'a respectable young farmer bearing the character of a very honest man' put in a bill for £133 10s. 6d. The first item on his bill was a sheep at £1 11s. 6d. which was an ewe of a special kind that regularly produced two lambs.[50] A young calf was valued at £1 5s. by Mortimer when purchased but Mathias had to value it at ten weeks old. The custom of the area apparently was to buy quantities of pork and beef when cheap and salt it down for winter and spring when prices rose. The furniture at Trehowel suffered considerably and one chair, reputedly used by Tate, was later repaired by the blacksmith at Pont Iago and is still in use today at a farm near Dinas.[51]

The owners of the *Molly* sloop from Ilfracombe sunk by the French were told not to expect anything as Mathias wasn't sure whether their claim came within the meaning of the Lord Lieutenant's letter.

The faithful Nesbitt meanwhile had a harder task. He was given a commissary post and made a return on 10 March of all the arms in the Quartermaster's stores at Haverfordwest and in the guard house at Fishguard. He must have been worried by the entry: '2 boxes of grenades missing and 20 muskets unserviceable,' but his neatly written returns were signed by General Rooke.

One of the unfortunate sufferers who does not seem to have come out of the affair with much fortune was Thomas Noot[52] who acted as surgeon to the Fishguard Fencibles. In May 1808 he wrote to Lord Castlereagh asking for his bill to be paid, presumably after writing to sundry other people in the 11 years since the events of 1797. His bill covered the French sick as well as some of the Fencibles and is interesting for its details and its faulty addition:

> Medical Services 22nd February - 29th March, 1797
> Attendance on sick   £ 8 18s.
> 20 men in Camp fever @ 6/8d   6 13s.
> 18 Pleurotic affections   4 -
> 18 Perpneumony @ 6/8   6 -
> 8 Diarrhoea   2 13 4
>   £ 38 4 8

Mr. Knight, Secretary of the Medical Board, refused to pay this and wanted proof that Dr. Noot had actually been surgeon to the Fencibles. Eventually after a further exchange of letters he agreed on a payment of 1d. per week per man over a period of 37 days. Presumably only the sick men could be charged for so that Dr. Noot had to be content with a mere £9 17s. 4d.

The business of clearing up afterwards was left largely to Colonel Knox. He found the sick men at Trehowel and a great quantity of arms and ammunition. Leaving Lieutenant Propert in charge with a small detachment he helped escort the arms to Haverfordwest.[53] He also prepared a casualty list. This was done on the spot and excludes any Frenchmen who might have been drowned in the boat that was lost and one man who was thrown over the cliff. Also left out was a Welsh woman accidentally killed by one of the Castlemartin Yeomanry in Fishguard, when he loaded his pistol in an inn:

Killed, as far as is known
 Dead bodies found near Trehowel   2
 Killed by country people   2
                                     Total 4
 Killed by French   2
                 Signed. Thos. Knox
                       Lieut. Col. Cmmnd.

John Mends of Haverfordwest gave an account of the scene in the local newspaper when the carts rolled in with the spoils of war:

> Early this morning [Monday 27 February] their arms arrived in thirty carts, amounting to about 19 hundred musquets[54] and bayonets, with the same number of Belts and Cartouches, Each containing 19 Rounds of Cartridge & Balls, and Several Kegs of Gunpowder and Boxes of musquet Balls, with about 18 Brass Drums & Some Flags with the Tree of Liberty painted on them.[55]

John Mends added as a PS to his letter:

> Since I wrote the above there is arrived in H.West from Fishguard 16 Carts Loaded with kegs of Gunpowder which the French hid in the caves of the Rocks there, and our people says that there is as much hid there which will be brought in tomorrow, and about 2 thousand Stand of arms hid in the Sand in Chests, which will be brought in also tomorrow. Those arms and amonition were intended to arm all the country people that would join the French ...
>
>   I long to get among them [The Baptists who were holding meetings every night outside Haverfordwest] but have not been able to quit this town. They have sent me an anonymous letter which I have treated with the contempt it deserves.[56]

Unfortunately there is no trace of this last letter but the local press was often republican in its politics and anyone caught paying too much attention to it was suspected of treason. There was a hatred of nonconformity in the Haverfordwest area, perhaps because it had always been an isolated pillar of the English church.

The Rev. John Reynolds, Baptist minister of Middle Mill near Solva was under suspicion for having collected a republican paper for a friend which he had failed to deliver. His house was searched but nothing was found so he was freed. The two men who had suffered most by the French were also suspected — William Thomas of Mathry, who had lost his watch and shoe buckles, and Thomas Williams who had escorted the two French officers into Fishguard and whose wife Mary had been maltreated by French soldiers. Both these two were released as soon as it was realised how they had suffered. Another man who had suffered at the hands of the French but was not immediately released was the Rev. Henry Davies of Llangloffan. He was out preaching when the French landed and made his way by a roundabout route with some servants and a cart to Panteurig on Thursday morning.[57] Leaving his cart out of sight he made his way to the house to discover the door open and seven muskets levelled at him. He was maltreated and robbed of everything but a halfcrown. He was locked up but managed to escape and tell his servants to dismantle the cart and hide the parts in the bushes so the French party, who were out looking for horses and carts, would not be able to find it. Eventually released, the Fishguard people still believed the rumour that he had been standing on a rock instructing the French how to land and the following year he was burnt in effigy in Fishguard.

An amusing example of the loyalty of the nonconformists at the time comes from Rhydybont Congregational Church in Carmarthenshire[58] where the news of the landing, greatly exaggerated, came by a messenger who arrived in the middle of morning service. A famous preacher, Rev. Hughes, stopped preaching and suggested Dafydd Shon Emwnt, the venerable minister, should say a prayer for them. This was done and silence descended once more to be quickly broken by one Nancy Jones who decided they should all die, in true Welsh style, singing. Whereupon she found a suitable hymn: *Os wyt Ti am ddybenu'r byd* (God if thou has determined to destroy the world, gather thine elect together and then do it) which was sung lustily by all present including the tongue-tied ministers. Rev. Hughes then finished his sermon.

The trials of Thomas John and Samuel Griffith, two local men arrested for making friends with the French, took place[59] in March with Richard Foley, Deputy Clerk to the Crown responsible for preparing the prosecution and several J.P.s — Henry Mathias, Barrett Bowen Jordan, William Bowen, Mayor Francis Edwardes — and an interpreter, C. Harris Sanxay, were also present as was General Rooke. Much has been made of the fact that some of the Frenchmen were called in to act as witnesses by the prosecution but as the two men were being tried for treason, in that they communicated and collaborated with the French, it is difficult to imagine who could have supplied evidence other than members of the French camp.

The Frenchmen called as witnesses were Charles Prudhomme, a Bostonian ex-mariner turned soldier, Francois L'Hanhard, who had been absent from the camp for some time, as messenger between Tate and Cawdor, Sergeant Major Binet, Corporal Gaspard Degouy, Grenadiers Ashet and Meille and Private Maltbé. John had apparently been seen in the French camp with a 'Horse with Cropt Ears', and holding a whip and a piece of paper on the day of the capitulation. All the witnesses agreed on the horse, which appears to have been produced as evidence (presumably outside the court) but few agreed on the time. John was supposed to have told Binet and others that half the British force were 'women in red flannels' and that there was no reason for them to surrender as a great many Welsh would join them.

According to his own story[60] he had got up at 6a.m. on the Thursday and rode the six miles to Fishguard with Moses Price. When they arrived they had followed the Fencibles to the Scleddau turnpike where they met John's landlord, Mr. Phelps. A few others joined them including George Woolcock, who had a glass (telescope) and could see people on top of Carne Coch near the French advance post. He thought they were Welsh so they went up to join them. When John and William Symmonds reached the top, having passed others going down, they saw 200 Frenchmen and an officer with a flag. They were seen and fired on so they descended and rode off to Trehylin farm where they spotted the French looting in small groups.

They then went to Moses Mathias's house near Scleddau where they fed their horses and John lent his to Thomas Jenkins of the Fencibles who was in need of a lift. When he reached Manorowen John met his neighbour James Bevan and went home as it was by then 6p.m. and very dark. The next day John rode in early and met Thomas, another friend and, at Manorowen, he heard Ensign Bowen of the Fencibles ask for a horse for someone to get some meat. Once more his horse was put to good use by Thomas Jenkins who came back with the sensational news of a dead Frenchman and a dead blacksmith at Pencaer.

John was obviously over-inquisitive for this was a sight he couldn't miss. He went up the hill with one William Lloyd of Castleyblythe and after seeing the two dead bodies, found he was in the French camp. Here Major Ackland rode up to him to ask him to urge the French on as they were preparing to march down to Goodwick to surrender. He asked the marching men why they had come to Wales. 'Tis Welch then in these parts' said one man. 'Was there any brandy or porter?' he was asked. John said he didn't know and were there any more of them coming over. The Frenchman said he thought there were as Brest was preparing for another expedition at the moment. Finally John bought two cutlasses for 6d. each and gave one to an old lady. He went home with Peter Neyler and Thomas Jenkins to Little Newcastle where he lived.

It was then the turn of Samuel Griffith to be tried. He was accompanied by Thomas Davies of Caswilia (who was tried later) when, the prosecution argued, he was seen at 10a.m. on Thursday the 23rd in the field above Trehowel by Francois L'Hanhard. He was asked how many troops there were in Fishguard, to which he replied 'Not many' and L'Hanhard had said that he was not to be afraid because they only came to fraternize, to which Griffith had said he knew. Griffith had a beard and the next witness, Captain Bertrand said he thought that he had seen a man similar to Griffith but with a darker beard talking to L'Hanhard.[61]

Two Welshmen, James and John Rees, gave evidence that they had heard Griffith repeat the remark that the French had not come to do any harm. There had been an argument and Griffith had said he 'would fight for his King while he had life.'

Thomas Davies said he had gone on the Thursday to Pencaer with his brother-in-law Thomas Skeel and they had met John Evans of Trefayog, whose farm had been plundered so all three went to assess the damage. Griffith in his statement said he had not been in the field above Trehowel on the 23rd but had set out for St. Nicholas where he had been warned away and, with three neighbours, had climbed Tre-llys to watch the events. Before this he had sent ten men with the only gun in his house to join the peasantry at Goodwick. On the 24th Griffith had joined up with Davies and made for Carne Coch accompanied by his son. Although this was the day of the surrender and some of the French were giving away their arms, a large crowd of Frenchmen surrounded them and took them to Trehowel. Davies got there first and was taken by an officer to Tate, who asked him if he had come from the English Army. Davies had said he thought there was some mistake. Tate said he had had a letter from Lord Cawdor the night before and was preparing articles of surrender. Griffith then came into the parlour to see Davies on one side of the fire and Tate on the other. Davies was drinking a glass of brandy and they were shortly both given an escort to see them out of the French lines. Near Brestgarn they met Barry St. Leger, who said he had quarrelled with Tate the night before and did they know how he could get to Ireland. Griffith suggested he had better go back and surrender his arms.

Davies seems to have been acquitted at once but the depositions of John and Griffith were sent to London. In April at the Great Sessions in Haverfordwest the two men were bound over for trials for high treason. Once more in jail, the only thing that could now save them would be a flaw in the witnesses statements. This occurred in an unexpected way. Charles Prudhomme decided to tell John Rees, a fellow prisoner, that he had been offered money to the amount of 60 guineas 'to swear a lie against him' (John). His statement was witnessed by three people and sent to Thomas John. Griffith was also sent a similar note.

About this time the Duke of Rutland visited the prison and remarked that the French prisoners seemed happy and that he didn't think that John and Griffith would be hanged. On the day of the Assizes there was considerable excitement in Haverfordwest. Two leading barristers, Mills and Blackstone, were engaged for the defence and Richard Foley acted for the prosecution. Mills in opening the cross examination scored a mark against the case

Thomas John's headstone at Little Newcastle. He was arrested and tried for collaboration with the French, but acquitted. However, he died aged 38 as a result of being taken ill whilst in prison

59

for the prosecution. L'Hanhard, who was living in lodgings, had been suspected of stealing three silver spoons. Mills showed him a spoon and 'this had a visible effect on him. It cut the comb of his impudence.' He said he had seen it before and Prudhomme had accused him of stealing it but Prudhomme was a liar. Meille and Degouy refused to give evidence and Ashet said he had seen someone on a horse but it was not necessarily John. Binet confirmed John's deposition. The judge seems to have been disappointed and cautioned John that he should be more careful in future and should the French land again 'all traitors must be got rid of.' The jury was asked to acquit both men and this they did to the joy of Griffith's and John's many friends and relations present.

Fenton summed up the farcical nature of the trial in his book on Pembrokeshire when he said 'I may venture to ask how it were possible for such men without fortune, learning or connections to give effect to their principles, malignant as they might have been, and communicate with foreigners in an unknown tongue, who scarcely knew the patois of their own.'

There were others like Griffith and John, who out of sheer curiosity and excitement went out of their way to see the French. Once such was a Mr. Jenkins, who was at Merthyr Tydfil when he first heard about the French landing.[62] It was Friday evening and he did not really believe it until Sunday night when his servant reported the road — he was now back at home near Hay-on-Wye — choked with troops. On Tuesday he set off for Brecon where he had breakfast as the last troop of the Romney Dragoons was leaving. He caught up with them at Llandovery, where he heard they were ordered back as the French had surrendered. Undeterred he went to Carmarthen where he stayed at the Ivy Bush, the main inn in the town where the French officers were held. On 1 March there was alarm and confusion after a rumour of another landing, and Lord Dynevor's Carmarthenshire Yeomanry with their swords drawn and pistols loaded, marched the French officers off to the local jail. Jenkins however, at 7a.m., saw Colonel Tate being taken to the jail. 'He was a tall thin old man about 60, was dressed in a long blue Coat faced with Scarlet, blue Pantaloons, white waistcoat, Cocked Hat and National Cockade.'

At 8a.m. news came in from Kidwelly that there had been a landing on the Gower peninsula. This caused 'utter consternation the Townspeople assembling and the Country people coming in with what Guns, Musketts and Arms they could raise; and the officers learning them their exercises

... At 10 o'clock the Mail Coach arrived, and when they left Swansea early in the morning all was quiet, and they had heard nothing of the French landing in Gower.' There was one passenger on the coach, a Mr. Shaw taking despatches to Lord Cawdor and General Rooke. Jenkins talked to him and joined him in the coach which went on towards Carmarthen. On the way they met Lord Cawdor and General Rooke so Shaw joined them and left Jenkins alone in the coach. Jenkins used the opportunity to send a guard — perhaps the man on top of the coach with a blunderbuss — to get a Frenchman's cap for 2s. At Milford Haven he went to the hospital where there were 12 French soldiers 'as was sick'. He made his way in and bought them a drink for 5s., getting some 'Silver for their Silver and Copper money.'

The following day he left for home and was questioned at Brecon about his caps, which he describes as: 'made of leather, something like our Lighthorseman's Caps, with black Horse Hair along the top and falling down to one side, and traced over the Scull-cap with narrow strips of Tin'd Iron. I had the two Caps strapped before me on the Sadle, and they something resembled a pair of Pistol Holsters. Arrived ... home after a pleasant journey of 107 miles and back in 4 days.'

The most interesting thing about Jenkins' account is the ease with which he managed to communicate with the prisoners.

One other to face a serious charge as a result of the 'invasion' was Colonel Knox, for he was accused of cowardice.[63] On 21 March at his home at Minwere he heard that Major Williamson had been 'sent down to examine into his conduct.' The Major, a regular soldier, was sent by General Rooke as a result of a letter from Charles Hassall, his father's dismissed steward who had seen him retreating to Haverfordwest. Williamson showed Knox Hassall's letter: 'Mr. Vaughan is governor of the fort at Fishguard and complains loudly of the cowardly conduct of Colonel Knox'. Hassall wrote, setting out Knox's actions, stating the bombardiers refused to spike their guns and that he, Hassall, was the first to stop Knox retreating; 'but the young gentleman thought it more prudent to provide for the safety of himself and abandon the town and neighbourhood to their fears and their foes.'

Vaughan was not amused at his name being used and wrote to Knox saying that: 'Hassall had been writing a pack of stuff to MacNamara and he, I find, has been telling the Duke of York [commander-in-chief of the British army].' John MacNamara, a well known barrister had done some land dealings with Lord Cawdor in 1794 and had met Hassall at the time.[64] He held the large estate of Biddleston Park, on the Buckinghamshire–Northamptonshire border. In 1784 he had been MP for Leicester and four years later was Colonel of the Westminster Volunteers. He also owned a large estate on the Wye and in forwarding Hassall's letter pledged 'his life, his honour and his fortune on the veracity.'

Lord Cawdor was probably approached by Hassall over the same subject, for an interesting, undelivered draft letter survives concerning Knox. It is addressed, on the inside only, to the Duke of York:[65]

> I lament feeling myself under the heartfelt necessity of reporting to your Lordship R.H. the total want of discipline and unsoldierlike appearance of the corps of Fishguard Volunteers commanded by Lieut. Col. Knox which your R.H. may believe to be most glaring when confronted with the steadfastness appearance of younger corps whose expense to the Government was comparatively trifling. [The cost of paying the troops for the three days was £24 11s. 2d. and included 4 pints of beer for every man per 24 hours.] I think it my duty to inform your R.H. that the task confined on Mr. Knox, a very young man without experience or influence in the county, has to my knowledge prevented many old officers and gentlemen in the counties of Pembrokeshire and Cardiganshire from offering their services for the supplementary Militia, Provisional Cavalry or Volunteer companies.

A first class row was now brewing and one feels sorry for Lord Milford, who, when Knox was told he couldn't have a Court Martial at which he intended to clear his name, sent him a brief letter, no doubt as ordered:

> Sir,
> I am sorry to be under the necessity of signifying to you his Majesty's wish that you would resign your command of the Fishguard Fencibles. His Majesty is, however, perfectly well satisfied with your conduct, courage, and loyalty, shewn on a late occasion. I am, Sir,
> Your very humble servant etc MILFORD
> London, May 13, 1797

Two days later, possibly ignorant of Lord Milford's letter, Lieut. Gen. Rooke received a round robin from a deputation of 19 Militia officers[66] who all resigned their commissions in a carefully thought out sentence:

> We think it our duty to apprize you that the regard we feel due to our own reputations as officers must force us into the painful necessity of resigning the Commissions we have at present the honour to hold rather than under any circumstances risk our characters by acting under the command of Lieut.-Col. Knox whose ignorance of his Duty & want of judgment must be fully known to you.[67]

Knox was unexpectedly supported by Colby who gave a long account of his movements on the 22nd to General Rooke.[68] In Knox's account he states that Colby suggested he should retreat. In Colby's words, written in the third person, a different version of events is set out:

> That Lieut. Col. Colby staid in the Fort about half an hour and then told Lt. Col. Knox he should then go back to H.Wt. and would return again with the Troops from thence to his support with the utmost expedition ... That during the time he conversed with Lt. Col. Knox in the Fort he appeared perfectly collected nor did Lt. Col. Knox shew any signs of timidity but on the contrary recollects in conversing with him that he intimated as if he intended to move out to attack the enemy when his Newport Division had joined him ...

Colby then relates how surprised he was that on the march from Haverfordwest he learnt that Knox was 6 miles from that town. He asked Knox 'if the Enemy had appeared in such force as to occasion' his retreat. Colby couldn't remember Knox's exact words but did recall he had been informed the French had captured Fishguard. Colby sent Edwardes and Phillipps forward to see if this was true and they came back saying that the enemy hadn't moved from Pencaer.

This account from Colby appeared to satisfy the easy going General Rooke, who reckoned, on Williamson's advice, that his retreat was due to want of judgment rather than cowardice. However there had been another witness to Knox's movements who seemed to agree with Hassall. This was a Mr. Williams, who may have been the Rev. John Williams of Begelly who lived in Fishguard. He wrote, very caustically, to the Secretary at War in London:[69]

Sir,

    Economy is the cry of the day, which if not shortly adopted, the nation is ruined. All Forts except those that protect our docks are useless. We have one here which might well be spared: instead of protection it might have proved our ruin. For on the Enemy's first debarcation, our worthy Governor was missing, and neither seen, or heard of, till they had laid down their arms. The Fort was abandoned, and his brave Garrison (the like troops the world never saw) were found straying in Treffgarne forest, the next day at noon, where possibly they might have wandered as long as the Israelites did in the Wilderness had not the Pembroke fencibles luckily picked them up on their march from Haverfordwest to Fishguard. The French wanted nothing but Artillery and Ammunition to burn and destroy this country, here they might have had both without the least resistance, so for God's sake, if you chuse to let the fort stand, take away the Cannon which can never be of any service to us, but may be cursedly mischievous in the hands of the Enemy.

    I am right honourable Sir,

    Your devoted humbles servant,

    J. (or T.) Williams, Clerk

Right Honourable William Windham, Secretary at War, Whitehall.

On 24 March General Rooke had a letter, possibly as a result of the above and of Hassall's letter, from Colonel Brownrigg, the Duke of York's secretary, saying that His Royal Highness was satisfied with Knox's conduct and Williamson could return to Bristol. Knox, who resigned on 17 March, was still determined to obtain justice. He wrote to Lord Cawdor on the 18th asking for a copy of the letter that had been signed by the 19 officers. Lord Cawdor replied by return giving the reasons for his resignation as 'my conviction of your inexperience, and ignorance of your duty, joined to want of judgment.'[70] Knox was hurt by this haughty reply, so hurt in fact that he wrote at once challenging Lord Cawdor to a duel. He suggested it should be 'on this side of Pembroke ferry' and that his friend Col. Dan Vaughan would be his second.

Lord Cawdor received this astonishing piece of news on the 23rd and hardly mentions it in his diary, so we don't know what actually occurred.[71] Certainly he replied in his usual suave, matter-of-fact, manner saying that he had detained Knox's servant three hours while he contacted 'a friend', his ADC Joseph Adams, who would be his second and suggested they met at midday 'upon the turnpike road between the Pembroke Ferry and the road that turns off to Williamston.'

There is no record that they did actually meet. Knox had gone from his house at Llanstinan near Fishguard to his 'chateau of Minwere', as a fellow Militia officer called it, which is on the Eastern Cleddau. Both men would have to take ferries and it is possible that after they met, the seconds calmed Knox down because Lord Cawdor 'rode home all alone back by ½past one' and then went out riding with his wife, whom he always called Car, in Cheriton park near Stackpole. This means that he could not have spent more than a few minutes with Knox as the distance from Williamston to Stackpole is at least 9 miles and one doesn't know exactly how long the ferry journey home would take, but half an hour would be a fair estimate. He had to say goodbye to Adams and it is unlikely that the rest of his journey could take much less than an hour so one comes to the conclusion that he could not possibly have had time to fight a duel. The day was hot and, as Tate had discovered, Pembrokeshire on a fine day makes one feel more inclined to sleep than to fight.

Knox called in his father to help, but the old man, once an important figure in America, no longer had any influence and was unable to obtain copies of the necessary letters as evidence. Knox junior then wrote his curious but fascinating book, which is mostly a collection of letters, entitled: *Some account of the proceedings that took place on the landing of the French near Fishguard, in Pembrokeshire, on 22nd February 1797; and of the inquiry held afterwards into Lieut. Col. Knox's conduct on that occasion by order of His Royal Highness the Commander in Chief.*

The stables at Lard Cawdor's estate at Stackpole. The house was dismantled in the 1960s having been damaged by the Army during the war

Every available piece of evidence to hand to further his good conduct is included. There is a long account of what took place when a privateer, *Le Dauphin*, commanded by an émigré, M. La Robrie, put into Fishguard and Knox went to assist in the taking in of stores. Also included is a letter from William Fortune, who states that: 'I was requested by the Committee (of which Lord Milford, the High Sheriff for the County [Mr. Nathaniel Phillips of Slebech], the Mayor, and Captain Scourfield formed a part) on the morning of the landing of the French troops at Pencaer, to go to Fishguard, and inform you that they thought it most advisable for you to retreat towards Haverfordwest.'[72]

The only real evidence against Knox was that he abandoned the fort and retreated before he met Fortune. Luckily Ensign Bowen had carried off the powder and ammunition but, had the French known the fort was abandoned, they could have sailed round some of their grenadiers and captured both fort and town with ease. Colonel Gwynne Vaughan wrote to the Duke of Portland about this on 25 February saying that had the French anchored in the harbour his fort would have been battered to pieces because he only had three rounds left for his eight nine-pounders. He had very little powder and the fort was 'defenceless for want of it.'

This situation was somewhat similar in Swansea when there was a rumour of an invasion on the Gower peninsula. Captain Davis called out the Swansea Royal Volunteers and 'ordered what drums we had to beat.' Unfortunately there was only one serviceable drum but a number of men turned up and within quarter of an hour were issued with ball cartridges. They were marched a mile or two but the portreeve refused to let them have any arms from the guard house as he had not been ordered to by the Lord Lieutenant, so poor Captain Davis was in a very difficult position. The jealous portreeve subsequently claimed he had assembled the men and given them arms and that Davis was not doing his duty. The luckless Captain was dismissed and on 23 March Lieut. Col. Landes and Major William Jones took over the Volunteers.[73]

Whilst the charges against Thomas John and Samuel Griffith may appear trumped up, that there spies around is proven by a report from an unknown man in Cardigan that reached Paris on 6 March where it was printed in *Le Moniteur*, one of the official revolutionary journals:

16 Ventose An V.

Debarquement de 1400 Français sur la tote du comte de Pembrock. Marche de trois mille paysans ayant le lord lieutenant a leur tête avec un regiment de volontaires. Prise de ces 1400 hommes quin'ont oppose aucune résistance. Details de cet evénement contentu dans une letter de Cardigan: le correspondant declare que d'après leur conversation, il a compris qu'ils étaient de ci-devant soldats de Charette at de Stofflet, mêles avec des bandits de Bocage.[74]

The report then goes on to say that the public funds had reached an all time low and bank payments had been stopped. The French probably shrugged their shoulders, this was nothing new, the Assignat was virtually worthless.

In the meantime, it took a while for matters to return to normal in Pembrokeshire. Fishguard people who had at first left town, came home quickly, but Richard Fenton, the historian, said he had a child at Goodwick he did not hear about for three days.

Major Bowen of the Fencibles, who lived at Llwyngwair on the Cardigan-Fishguard road, had a long letter from his son in Bath which is typical of the concern shown by those with relatives in 'French-occupied' Pembrokeshire:

> My very honoured and affectionate father,
> An account just reached Bath [he wrote on 26 February] that a French force of 1200 men had landed between St. Davids and Fishguard, but happily for my own anxiety the number is said to have been landed from so small a force as two frigates and a lugger, made it appear so improbable that I would not give credit to it, until about half an hour afterwards I met a Gentleman who showed me a letter he had received from Laugharne confirming the acct. of the number, accompanied by the happy tiding of their having surrendered and the ships having quitted the coast — no doubt my poor dear mother and sister must have been much alarmed, and altho' I trust their apprehension of danger is now subsided, I shall not be easy in my mind till I hear from you. Pray send me a line ...
> Geo Bowen[75]

George Bowen finished by stating that he would have 'gloried in the opportunity of exercising arms for the protection of his family.' He did not realise that his friends in neighbouring Bristol very nearly had to spring to arms to fight this force, which had it landed where it was originally supposed to land, might have used its incendiary supplies to greater advantage.

7   The Prisoners & Further Alarms

If the prisoner is happy, why lock him in?
If he is not, why pretend that he is?
George Bernard Shaw, *Man and Superman*

French prisoners of war in Britain at this time were mostly housed in prisons near the coast, which meant that their chances of escaping, especially at Portchester, were high once they had got out of their prison. The news that Tate had nearly landed in Bristol got to Stapleton Prison there and produced a riot. A sentry fired and killed one of his own comrades and mop-sticks were made into pikes by the prisoners. There were over 1,000 prisoners and the situation looked so serious that for a time the Bristol authorities even considered lowering them down the Kingswood coalpit.

Whilst the men under Tate's command had been imprisoned in Haverfordwest, the officers had been sent to Carmarthen where they were lodged in the town jail for a time, *The Times* stating that they had even been allowed to retain their swords. However, they proved unpopular with the local inhabitants. Mayor Edwardes wrote to the Duke of Portland, the Home Secretary, whose intray concerning the invasion must have overflowed his desk, saying that 'if they are left in this country inevitable ruin must follow. The loyalty of the people here is beyond description. We have too many French Officers here. Your Grace would render us essential service if they were sent farther into the country. Hereford and Brecon are two proper places.'[76]

Another correspondent, Mr. Lloyd, wrote to his MP, John G. Philipps c/o Strand Coffee House, London on 2 March suggesting that the French officer prisoners should be moved at once away from the harbour. He then changed the subject completely, a surprisingly common habit amongst 18th-century Welsh letter writers, and asked Mr. Philipps to choose him a cutlass with trimmings. 'I think,' he concluded, forgetting all about prisoners, 'a morocco belt would be stronger or better than silk.'[77]

The exaggerations of Knox and Lord Cawdor about the thousands of troops at their command was nearer the truth than they themselves knew. The roads to Pembrokeshire were now crowded with the militia and rumours of new landings kept up the pressure. Colonel Deering's New Romney Fencible Cavalry were summoned from Worcester and four troops arrived in record time at Haverfordwest to help escort the prisoners when they were moved. The Breckon Volunteers under Captain Henry Allen had reached Llandovery before they were told of the surrender.

Meanwhile at Pembroke in the infamous Golden prison there were already 500 prisoners and Mr. Mansell, the Commissiary, posted up to London on 15 March to see about an increase in his emolument if he now took a larger number of prisoners. Colonel Knox in his account suggests that the reason for the French attack was to liberate these prisoners but nothing specifically had been stated about them in Tate's orders, beyond the fact that liberated prisoners should be armed by their liberators.

After a brief stay at Haverfordwest, where St. Mary's church was considerably damaged inside, the unwelcome prisoners, or most of them, were ferried across the Cleddau to Pembroke and put in Golden prison.

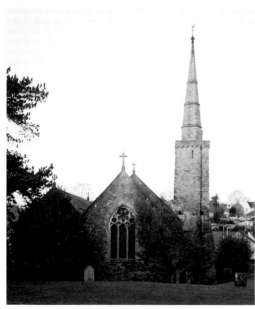

Among them were the young Marquis de Saint-Amand and a grenadier sergeant called Roux, who planned a breakout. Two young girls, Anne Beach, the sister-in-law of the Rev. James Thomas of Haverfordwest and her friend Eleanor Martin brought the French their provisions in covered pails and baskets. Soon they had fallen for these two handsome Frenchmen and agreed to help them. By using meat bones the prisoners dug a 60ft.-long tunnel under the wall using the baskets and pails to remove the unwanted earth.[78]

St. Mary's Church, Haverfordwest,
where many of the prisoners were initially held

The entrance to Pembroke harbour under the walls of the castle

By mid-July all was ready and early one morning 31 Frenchmen escaped and hurried to the harbour guided by the two girls. One man decided to make his own way and was subsequently recaptured. The others rushed to a sloop in the harbour, which proved to be aground, but nearby they found a small yacht that belonged to Lord Cawdor. Commandeering this, they sailed out of the harbour with the provisions found on the sloop and then captured a brig off Linney Head by pretending to be ship-wrecked sailors. The crew were put below except for the helmsman who was forced to set sail for St. Malo which they reached a few days later. The yacht, meanwhile, had been cast adrift and pieces of it, including the name board, were found in Milford Haven shortly after the event. The Marquis later married Anne Beach.

The unfortunate Ensign Cole, in charge of the prison guard, wrote to his superior officer describing the events.

> 18th July, 1797
>
> I am sorry to inform you that on Tuesday morning last 31 of the French prisoners effected their escape. Three parties were sent out immediately and I have not the least doubt of their being retaken.
>
> I hope their escape will not be imputed to any neglect of mine as the Commissiary as well as myself did all in our power to guard against such an unforeseen accident.[79]

In August the remaining prisoners were shipped to Portsmouth. Writing at a later date describing the scene that day, the Duke of Rutland says in his journal.[80]

Monday — This morning we all paraded before eight o'clock, in order to be present at the embarkation of some of the French prisoners, taken in the late expedition. Lord Cawdor went on before to meet his troop, and the others of the party set off on horseback about eight to join him. The morning although it at first threatened, turned out very fine, and we had a delightful ride to Pembroke. Here we found the troops assembled (the same who had borne so glorious a share of the business at Pencaurn), and we underwent the ceremony of introduction to the several officers of the different corps. This done, we rode to the French prison, and went into it. It was a bad place for prisoners; as had the men chosen, they might easily have made their escape. As the treatment they experienced there, under the eye of Lord Cawdor was such, as to satisfy them perfectly, they were rather sorry at their removal, which was to be to Portsmouth. They knew the difference of treatment they would experience there, and although they stood a greater chance of a speedy exchange, they were not satisfied with their removal. Thirty of them had some time before broke loose from the prison, and taking a fine large pleasure boat of Lord Cawdor's escaped to sea. Off the land's end they boarded a brig, of which they took possession, and turning the yacht adrift, reached France in safety. Their leader (an Irishman), was afterwards retaken in a privateer, on board of which he had embarked. The prison exhibited a scene of noise and confusion scarcely to be equalled. The natural ease of the French character was most conspicuously evident. Unconcerned at their own fate, they were happy at the idea of novelty (bad as the change was to be for them), and were laughing and dancing about, with their knapsacks and bedding on their shoulders, ready to march. Some of them had a number of nicknacks of their own making, and some had white rabbits, which they had carefully preserved throughout all their dangers and difficulties. There were one or two very gentle looking men amongst them, but the generality were noisy and turbulent. Amongst them were two or three officers of low degree, one of them a Monsieur St. Amand, who during his stay at Haverfordwest, had so captivated a young lady of some fortune (by name Miss Beach) that she had consented to correspond with him by letter in his prison, and intends as we afterwards heard to marry him. Our entrance on horseback into the prison afforded an excellent fund of conversation to them. Lady Cawdor was dressed in a riding habit of the same uniform as her Lord's cavalry wore. Ah ! cried they, 'Sacre matin. Des dragons comme ca. Ce'st trop en verite.' Her horse had covering over its ears, as a guard against the flies. 'Regardez donc,' they cried, 'voyez les fausses oreilles. Comme c'est drole.' Thus they went on passing remarks on the whole company. Gascons, Normans, and people of every part of France were mixed together, and the different accents and noises, gave us a conception of the Tower of Babel. As soon as all was ready, the gates were thrown open, and they began their march. The escort consisted of about 200 men of different corps, and formed a parallelogram, in the middle of which they marched. Their number amounted to 154 men, and two women. They originally brought over four women, but two of them made their escape in Lord Cawdor's pleasure boat [Rutland was wrong here, as it was the two Pembrokeshire girls who escaped]. One of the prisoners was missing, and could not be found. Their march was about three or four miles to Pembroke Ferry, which is upon Milford Haven. The road was lined with many spectators, who were anxious to see the last of their invaders. Women, men, and children, crowded to see them, while they marched in the middle of their escort, laughing and singing the whole way. It was a pretty sight to see them winding up the hills before us, and along the turnings of the road, while the arms of the troops were glittering in the sun. Lady Cawdor and her party followed in the rear. On a sudden we came in sight of that glorious piece of water, Milford Haven; together with several vessels which were at anchor, or sailing about. The brig which was to transport the Frenchmen, had her sails unfurled, and was lying ready to receive them. As soon as the cavalcade was perceived winding round the hill, which brought them to the shore at the Ferry, several boats with some marines, put off from the vessel towards the land for them. The Haven is about half a mile broad in this part. When we arrived on the beach, the troops formed a half circle, reaching at either end to the water side, and the prisoners embarked from the middle, in the several boats, to the number of fifty in each. It was an interesting sight, to see the boats on their way to the vessel which lay at a short distance, while the troops remained under arms, attending the embarkation of those very men whom they had some time before taken prisoner. The mob of peasantry stood on the hill above, or lined the shore. About half past ten they were all on board. In the last boat, a civil Frenchman, whose life Lord Cawdor had saved, when he was in the act of sinking beneath a Welchman's blow, got up from his seat, and pulling off his hat, made two or three bows of gratitude to his deliverer, whom he spied on shore, at the head of his troops. The other boats were noisy and clamorous. This man particularly caught my attention, as he really appeared (and Lord Cawdor afterwards told me he was) a very quiet, civil kind of man. As soon as they were all embarked, Lady Cawdor went round and shewed herself to the troops, and we then returned to Pembroke, where we saw the men dismissed. Before we left the town, we took a view of the castle, Lady Cawdor and the Miss Campbells accompanying us to it. Lord Arthur finding himself unwell, rode home with Mr. King. The town itself is small and miserable. It stands on the edge of a hill, at the end of which is the castle, overlooking a precipice, which reaches down to a branch of the Haven. The architecture is chiefly Norman, together with some Gothic. The tower looks very well from every point of view, and is completely mantled with ivy. The height of this tower is 75 feet, and its walls are 14 feet thick. It is quite perfect, and even the stone vaulted roof remains. It has a noble appearance, when seen from a little distance towering above the Haven. With some difficulty, Hayes, Lord Cawdor, Mr. Edwards, and myself, ascended the tower by a broken staircase, led by the proprietor, a Mr. Meyrick, who lives at a place called Bush, near Pembroke. The ladies not wishing to rival us in feats of activity, remained at an humble distance below. We were not however repaid for our trouble as we gained no view by it. We now all returned towards Stackpole, pursuing a pleasant road across the fields. The day was very hot, and the sun shone bright. The sea was in view for a considerable time, forming an interesting scene. We entered Lord Cawdor's domain along the side of a very beautiful glen, whose sides were covered with fine woods; the only wood of any conse-quence about the place. In these, there are many pheasants, whose breed Lord Cawdor has encouraged as much as possible. Before we went home, we rode some way through the wood, along a drive which is at present forming, and will be extremely beautiful, being in many places completely over-arched by the surrounding foliage. On our return, Lord Cawdor shewed us a number of helmets and swords which had been taken from the French; amongst others, Tate's own sword, which was very fine. [This sword is not, and never has been, in the Cawdor family's possession. It would appear the Duke of Rutland was shown another sword, for Tate's sword is anything but fine.] They were all extremely good and serviceable. Before dinner, we took a walk to see the new bridge that is building, and also the kennel, where we saw a very pretty pack of beagles. In our return to the house, we met a sergeant of the Cardigan Militia, who was come to inform Lord Cawdor that the man who had been missing in the morning was found. He had concealed himself the whole time in the prison, and when the coast was, as he thought, clear, attempted to escape by jumping the wall, but was discovered by two of the Cardigan regiment, and immediately sent on board the vessel. His chief reason for trying to escape was his fear of the other prisoners, who had sworn to murder him, for some offence he had committed. He was an Irishman. Lord Cawdor gave the men half-a-guinea a-piece, and a guinea to the sergeant. Besides this, ten shillings are allowed by Government for any prisoner who is caught in the act of escaping. We now retired to dress for dinner, which was always punctual at four o'clock. In the evening we had some delightful music from the elder of the Miss Campbells, who sings charmingly.

There were numerous alarms during the following months as many people considered Tate's force to be the first of a series of landings. One such alarm was caused by Mr. Roach of Llyther near St. Davids.[81] He was a farmer with fields scattered all over the coast. One evening he went to Maes-y-mwny to inspect some fields and when he descended the cliff he heard voices in a language he didn't understand. Going closer be could just make out the masts of a vessel close to the shore. He rushed home and gave orders for his livestock to be dispersed in every direction. He then went into St. Davids where the cathedral organist, Mr. Richardson, had a speedy horse and reached Haverfordwest in 45 minutes which, considering it was virtually dark and he had to go up and down hills, was good riding. Mayor Edwardes held a committee meeting and despatches were sent to Swansea and Milford Haven. It was considered the French prisoners in the area should all be shot.

Meanwhile other people from St. Davids, perhaps some who knew Mr. Roach well, went to the shore and discovered a few coasters sheltering under Gessail Fawr filling up their water casks from a little stream. In later years more people spoke of 'French Roach Lleithyr' than of 'French Pencaer'. The only casualty of this costly scare, for messages were sent far and wide and troops assembled before later messages reached them that

75

it was a scare, was Mr. Richardson's horse. After '16 miles and 16 hills' it rolled over and died.

Another false alarm occurred on the first Sunday in March when, after the issue of a royal proclamation for a day of thanksgiving, all the inhabitants of Fishguard were in church. A messenger, no doubt from Mr. Williams of Trelethin or Mr. Tucker, came in without ceremony and said the French ships were coming back. With scenes of complete pandemonium, women fainting and men dashing about collecting their wits and their arms, people rushed out of the chapels and churches and assembled on Fishguard beach: 'resolved to conquer or to die when the squadron entered the bay.'[82]

The guns in the fort were loaded and fired, but in salute not in anger. The squadron flew the British colours and the ships were recognised as truly British. It answered the salute and an officer from *Indefatigable*, flagship of Sir Edward Pellew of the Plymouth squadron, landed to enquire after the fate of the invaders.[83] Pellew sailed up the coast to New Quay where a boat from the *Greyhound*, commanded by his brother Israel, landed to enquire into another rumoured invasion which in effect was a Liverpool convoy. In a report to Evan Nepean at the Admiralty, Pellew said that he had been informed the French ships had gone to Ireland and that he would follow, but he had despatched the *Stag* cutter to Admiral Sir Richard King at Falmouth to reinforce the defences there.

On his return trip the *Shannon* was sent into Milford to help escort the French prisoners to Spithead and the Admiral returned to Plymouth. Captain Fraser of the *Shannon* took over the organising of the embarkation of both men and officers.

Further up the coast at Hafod, the home of Thomas Johnes the wealthy Colonel of the Carmarthenshire Militia who lived in a remote spot near Aberystwyth, his wife, Jane Johnes was all alone. She accepted help from her nearest neighbour writing to him with news of yet another rumour: 'I have heard that the sail of the French are off Aberystwyth and Aberaeron. If you are able to, let me beg of you to come over and bring what arms you can and powder and shot; they will not sell any at Aberystwyth ... you need not bring any people with you. We have enough here if we had Arms.'[84]

When Lieut. General Rooke, Officer Commanding Severn District, arrived to take command of all the troops in the Pembroke area he reported to the Duke of Portland:

My Lord,   Haverfordwest, 3 March

In answer to your Grace's letter respecting the information which has been received of the condition of the French Prisoners taken in the County, I have to inform your Grace of the present disposal of them which I judge perfectly secure. Seven hundred are on board transports off Milford, 415 confined in this castle in this Town, 75 sick secured at Fishguard and 34 (styled officers) are in the jail at Carmarthen. Proper guards are furnished in each situation and I shall pay every attention to their being treated suitable to their condition.

Tate and the Irish officers St. Leger, Tyrrell, Morrison (whom Lord Cawdor calls Norris in his letters) and the second-in-command, Le Brun, left Carmarthen on 2 March after a difficult night because there had been a rumour of another landing in the Gower peninsula. Lord Cawdor and his faithful ADC Joseph Adams escorted Tate and Tyrrell in one carriage, he had Le Brun in another, because the future Baron de Rochmure had 'better manners' although 'as dirty as a pig'. The final carriage consisted of Rooke's ADC, Lord Edward Somerset, and Captain Morrison and Lieutenant St. Leger. The people watching were very indignant when they realised the French leaders were in the carriages but Lord Cawdor found his 'influence would protect them without difficulty.'

At Oxford where they spent the night the only guard they could obtain was a sergeant and two recruits. At Uxbridge the crowd thought Tate was Colonel Wall, a former Governor of Goree who had flogged a soldier to death when the man had asked for a pay rise, and the American was frightened stiff. By cutting through the parks the carriages avoided most of the London crowd. They reached the Duke of Portland's offices safely and for the first time Lord Cawdor, who was exhausted with the strain of responsibility and the long journey, was able to relax. He took the opportunity to write to the Duke of Portland:[85]

                                   Oxford Street, Sunday even
My Lord   March 5th, 1797

It being incumbent on me to explain to your Grace the situation in which I left the County of Pembroke, I shall recapitulate the outline of the late transaction, tho' not with sufficient detail to do justice to the extraordinary and general spirit, zeal and loyalty of individuals, which burst forth, and co-operated with every wish I expressed during the short period of my command ...

He then goes on to state that he had taken command after speaking to Lord Milford. He praises Colonel Colby and states that he met Knox retreating to Haverfordwest and 'required him to put himself under my orders and to return towards the enemy.' He praises the help and local information he had from Mr. Nesbitt of Fishguard and states 'it was obvious that the Fishguard battery was as useless for land operation as it had been to impede the disembarkation.' He says that 50 men could have prevented the landing but 'it was not possible to dislodge them from their position but it was easy to hem them in and cut off their supply.'

He praises the 'extraordinary efforts of the Sea Officers and Seamen' who helped get the prisoners to Milford for embarkation to Pembroke. He finishes by carefully covering his actions:

> Lieut.-General Rooke having approved the arrangements I had made, I left under his orders the persons in whom I had vested the responsibility of occasional services, and I judged it my duty upon your Grace to give full information and to explain my late situation in the County which I beg your Grace to explain to His Majesty. I shall wait your Grace's orders and have left my family in the country until His Majesty's pleasure shall be known.
>
> I have the honour to be
>
> Your Grace's obedient humble servant CAWDOR

In Bristol the *London Gazette Extraordinary* was reprinted in the 4 March edition of *Felix Farley's Bristol Journal* giving Lord Milford's letter describing the peasantry attacking the French with pikes and scythes and the brief letter from Lord Cawdor stating that he was too fatigued to write more at this time. The only comfort was Lord Milford's second letter about the prisoners being on the march to Haverfordwest and for true Englishmen a large advertisement on the same page for the Duke of Beaufort's well known hunter 'Apollo'.

In Portsmouth the guards were doubled, two regiments of Militia moved in and, after a riot in which one prisoner was shot, the Portchester prisoners were moved to the new prison at Stilton, Huntingdonshire. On 3 March *The Times* was saying that it would be sensible to brand all the fellows with a hot iron, send them back to France and tell them if they return they shall not be met with any mercy. Another more amusing writer said that the English sent their convicts to New South Wales, but the French evidently sent theirs to Old South Wales.

On 6 March *The Times* reported that the five officer prisoners 'underwent an examination at the Admiralty and yesterday they were re-examined by Mr. Ford (a Bow Street magistrate) and some members of the Privy Council. Tate, who stiled himself Commander in Chief and signed the articles of capitulation, proves to be a Scotsman, also Morrison.' Later, Faucon (Tate's ADC) arrived in London and went through the same series of interviews.

Tate was worried in case he was going to be sent back to America, but the authorities decided that there was no cause for treating him as anything other than an ordinary prisoner of war. In May, after a spell in London, where he was presumably lodged in the Tower, he was sent to Portsmouth and confined in the *Royal Oak* prison ship. Here he was able to witness the Spithead mutiny and, anxious to get back to Paris, he wrote to the Lords of the Admiralty suggesting that he should be exchanged for Sir Sydney Smith, the famous frigate captain who had been captured by the French.[86] This request was refused but in November 1798, after a brief spell in Portchester Castle, he was sent back to France on parole. (A few months after the prisoners had been shipped to Portchester, Lord Cawdor visited them. Leaving his horse at the barrier he spoke to the Governor and returning much later discovered that his horse had been stolen and eaten by hungry prisoners.)[87]

The Irish officers, Morrison, Tyrell and St. Leger, had good cause to be tried for High Treason. Owing to there being numerous ex-émigrés working for the British in France, who, if caught would be subject to the same charge, nothing was done and they were sent to the *Royal Oak* at the same time as Tate. The French women captured at Goodwick were also despatched here with their husbands. Morrison and Tyrell were returned to France on parole at the same time as Tate and, no doubt, were able to give the French authorities information on the state of Britain's defences. This must have occurred to the War Office, who probably considered that the expense of keeping them in England was more than the value of the information they had obtained when in captivity, regardless of the fact that they were English speakers and had been permitted to read newspapers.

St. Leger apparently had no desire to return to France. Transferred to Portchester at the same time as Tate he listened to prisoners telling of various escapes. Two men had got out in empty barrels, three had dressed up as English officers and simply walked out of the gate after a church service. Once out of the prison there was a useful contact called Thomas More at Folkstone, alias Captain Harman, who could arrange you a passage across to France for a suitable fee. St. Leger knew the opportunity to escape would turn up and he duly took it. Nothing further is known about him, but some 20 years later Sir Edward Mansel's widow, Mary, married a Colonel Barry St. Leger, late of the 34th Regiment of Foot. Sir Edward had been a prominent member of the Society of Sea Serjeants, a Pembrokeshire Jacobite group, and no doubt when he died in 1754 he had left his widow a handsome sum of money.[88]

8 Results in London & Elsewhere

'1 feel it my duty to deliver my opinion on a measure of high importance at all times, but which, at the present period, is becoming infinitely more interesting than ever.' Charles James Fox, 26 May, 1797

The news of the French landing had reached Tenby at dusk on the 23rd. The mayor sent John Upcoat out to sea in a skiff with a message for the captain of a brig who put in at one of the Somerset ports and took it to the nearest staging post. This message arrived in London on Saturday the 25th, but Captain Longcroft's message to Evan Nepean, Secretary to the Admiralty, had reached London the previous day and on the Saturday an announcement was made in the press about the invasion. There was a run on the Bank of England on the Friday and an immediate drop in the value of Bank of England stock from 134 to 129½, whilst 3% Consols dropped to 50½d., their lowest for some years.

Yet the invasion was received with surprise rather than shock amongst the nobility and Lord Glenbervie, who had been First Secretary for Ireland in 1794, has left us an account of the news[89] in his diary which indicates that, although the Bank crisis was heightened by the invasion, it had in fact started before 22 February.

> Feb. 27th 8am. Bruton Street. The gloom that prevails among all ranks and classes seems to increase every day. The Government cannot dispose of their new Exchequer Bills issued in anticipation of the late loan and the subscriptions to the loan have fallen under 10% discount, so that it is more in the interest of the original holders to forfeit the first payment they have made than to make good subsequent payments. The 3% (Consols) were in the course of last week at 51 and a fraction, lower than ever was known at any former period. A new loan is necessary but Pitt has not yet been able to negotiate it, and, as every incident in such

a state of things serves to increase the panic, general consternation was excited on Saturday by intelligence received from Lord Milford, Lord Lieutenant of Pembrokeshire, that in the evening of Wednesday 22nd three French frigates had appeared off the coast, from whence 1200 troops with 3,000 stand of arms had been landed at the little seaport town of Fishguard.

Yesterday despatches arrived from Lord Milford with an account that two parties of 300 and 1100 French had on the 24th surrendered to the peasants and supplementary Militia of the county and were then on their march to Haverfordwest. By other letters it appears that Lord Cawdor had been very active in putting himself at the head of the Militia.

Last night we had a great batch of Shakespeare ... Lady Margaret enlarged on the gross faults and absurdities of Shakespeare which put us all in such a rage. [The native characteristic of mixing the humdrum with the serious news is one of the delights of Lord Glenbervie's diary.]

A *London Gazette Extraordinary* was published giving Lord Milford's letters to the Duke of Portland and one from Lieut. Colonel Paul Orchard from Hartland Abbey, Devon.

Lord Cawdor wrote a short letter to the Duke of Portland (who never seems to have replied to any of his letters on the subject of invasion), which expresses more truthfully the strain of the previous days:

> The fatigue we have experienced will, I trust, excuse me to your Grace for not giving a more particular detail; but my anxiety to do justice to the officers and men I had the honour to command, will induce me to attend your Grace with as little delay as possible to state their merits and at the same time to give you every information in my power upon this subject.[90]

The *Annual Register* reports that the French chef who worked in the royal palace was given his notice. There is no evidence of spying and it was probably due to his bad cooking or to the fact that the king was embarrassed by the public reaction to his employing a Frenchman. George III, after being shot at in London a few years before when riding in his coach, had bravely appeared at the theatre the same night. Here was another crisis for him. On the Sunday morning at a few minutes after 8 o'clock he sat down at his desk in Windsor and wrote to Pitt, whom he was going to see a few hours later, but perhaps it was meant for Pitt's eyes only and the king did not want the rest of the Privy Council to see it. 'I suppose' he concluded, 'the predatory attack and landing in Pembrokeshire will rather add to the dismay of the timid; but I trust that cool firmness which used to be the national asset of Englishmen will again appear.'[91]

The Times on Monday announced that Mr. Shaw, the Government Messenger, was sent on Sunday to request that the king came to town and that it was the first time during his reign that George III had come up to London to do business on a Sunday. A Privy Council meeting was held at St. James's Palace. Apart from the king, there were present on this occasion William Pitt, the Duke of York, Lords Portland, Grenville, Spencer, the Earl of Chatham and the Marquis of Cornwallis.[92] The result of the meeting was sensational. For the first time since the 1745 rebellion all cash payments by the Bank of England were suspended until 'the sense of Parliament can be taken on that subject.'

On the following day Francis Martin, Secretary of the Bank of England published the following letter:

> The Governor, Deputy Governor, and Directors of the Bank of England think it is their duty to inform the proprietors of Bank Stock, as well as the Publick at large, that the general concerns of the Bank are in the most affluent and prosperous situation, and such as to preclude every doubt as to the security of its notes. The Directors mean to continue their usual discounts for the accommodation of the commercial interest, paying the amount in Banknotes, and the dividend warrants will be paid in the same manner.
> The Bank of England Feb 27th 1797.

Charles Fox, leader of the Whigs, did not take this news easily and on behalf of the opposition in Parliament said that: 'when he considered the magnitude of the subject he was astonished that the Minister had not entered into a minute statement of the circumstances which led to an event so calamitous and unprecedented.'[92]

Lord Wycombe, a radical peer and Irish landowner, took his seat in the Commons on 28 February for the first time for three years. He was not sworn in and had to sit under the gallery, but the event caused a stir. A rumour of a landing at Louth, Lincolnshire, was received and another that the French had captured Pembroke castle. There was a feeling of intense excitement in the Commons which demanded and obtained a debate on a motion for the appointment of a committee to examine the outstanding demands on the Bank. Fox made one of his long, fiery speeches in which he said that the country had been amused at the state of finance in France but had not expected to find themselves in the same situation. The French did not depend on commercial credit to the same extent as we did and 'their rash expeditions have not put an end to their energy.'

Wycombe thought the scheme was merely to 'cover a design of sending money to the continent to carry on the war' and he thought that the government measures would produce misery, high prices and bring on a 'train of evils with which the House was unacquainted.' Mr. Sheridan brought on an amendment to the effect that the committee should enquire into 'the causes which have produced the order of the council of the 26th instant.' This was defeated by 244 votes to 86 but the motion itself was carried and a committee of 15 members was chosen by secret ballot. On 1 March a further motion on the stoppage of cash payments being made the subject of a special committee was defeated, but the names were announced of the committee: W. Hussey, Charles Grey, W. Plumer, T. Powys, T. Grenville, William Wilberforce, J. Blackburn, T.B. Bramston, C. Bragge, Sir J. Mitford, W.W. Bird, J. Fane, I.H. Browne, Sir John Scott and Alderman Anderson. Sheridan suggested that Fox should be added but the vote against this was decisive: Yeas, 53; Noes 140.

A similar committee was set up in the House of Lords under the Earl of Chatham.

It was not until 28 March that the Commons debated the state of defence of the country. A Colonel Wood proposed that a Board of Naval and Military Officers should be appointed to investigate and make recommendations. In a carefully worded and well constructed speech he pointed out that the public alarm over the Bank crisis was occasioned largely because the French had successfully hovered off the coast of Ireland for three weeks and then returned home without trouble from the British fleet. Another expedition had landed and only proved the ineffectual state of the nation's defence. In 1785 a board had been set up to inquire into the nation's defence. In Queen Elizabeth's time a council of 'the united wisdom of her kingdom' had met to defend the country against the Armada, surely there was no wiser plan than to adopt this motion.

Mr. Dundas, Secretary of War, said the motion directly affected the Duke of York and the other military leaders and that if the king was asked to name a committee these would be the people appointed. For this reason the motion should be adjourned. Charles Fox said that he had the greatest respect for the Duke of York but 'this was not a time to give up anything that was necessary for the safety of the country out of compliment to any person.' He doubted that the naval affairs were in the best hands. He then sat down after one of his shortest speeches and the stage was set for Colonel Wood's strongest supporter, Colonel Fullarton, MP for Ayrshire.

William Fullarton, described in 1779 as a 'hungry Scotsman willing to do anything he is paid to do' was a real fire-eater.[93] He had drawn up a plan to invade Mexico with four privateers in 1780 and had then raised his own regiment to do this. He had fought with distinction in India and returned to become MP for Ayrshire and, like Tate, he had imagination and a gift of the gab. 'It was essential,' he said 'that they [the House] should give to the public mind an impression that they were to be defended. Unfortunately the impression of late had been directly the reverse. In various parts the people conceived they were not sufficiently defended. To this impression was owing much of the calamity which had fallen the Bank of England and also the country banks ... every district should be put on such a footing of internal defence, as should enable us to give the French a proper reception on shore as often as they failed to be properly saluted by our squadrons at sea.'

Mr. Sheridan then said there had been no communication between the army and the navy in combining efforts to defend the country. Bantry Bay had been 'an instance of deplorable neglect.' Mr. Windham, Secretary at War and responsible for the day to day conduct of it (Dundas was more of a civil servant in the War Office), said that the motion would have to be dropped as the only result if it was passed would be that a committee would be formed of those people already chosen to defend the country. The debate was consequently adjourned.

One of the more surprising results of the invasion was the scheme of Dundas's secretary, Huskisson, to launch an attack on the Mexican coast. An army from the Cape of Good Hope commanded by an independently minded character called James Craig was to embarrass America by invading, Tate style, on the west of North America, to draw off American ships from the east. It was a mad scheme inspired by someone who had a personal grudge against America — he was not alone as the 1812 War was not far away.

A fanciful drawing of a possible invasion by balloon, tunnel and barge. Napoleon's actual plans were far simpler than this, based on a brief command of the Channel

Napoleon, meanwhile, had realised that a small landing was useless and only a large one could succeed. General Hoche, who no longer had command of the channel army, died in September 1797 in mysterious circumstances and the Directory lost its main driving force for invading Britain. Napoleon persisted, however, although his schemes for 1798 were spoilt by Admiral Duncan, who defeated the Dutch fleet at Camperdown.

Another manifestation of invasion rumour — a huge barge powered by windmills

However the French army of that year consisted of 275,000 men, whilst in Britain there were 32,000 regulars and a Militia of, on paper, 100,000 men. A French officer named Muskeyn invented a shallow boat fitted with a small gun firing forward. Orders were given for hundreds to be built. Rumours spread of a huge barge 2,000ft. long and 1,500ft. broad propelled by windmills. It reputedly could carry two divisions with artillery and cavalry and a later model, to be built at Dieppe; would have Mr. Fulton's revolutionary steam engine to drive it. An article in the *Gentleman's Magazine*[94] said it needed 216,000 trees to build it and would weigh 44,000 tons. Cartoons appeared showing it as a vast, clumsy tool of Napoleon's underfed army.

Meanwhile in Somerset the coast was fortified. Hannah More wrote to a friend from near Bristol saying: 'Our most respectable friends were forming Volunteer corps at their own expense ... gunboats are stationed and fortifications erected.'[95]

In Milford Haven, however, there was still no proper defence system and a Lieutenant Allen R.N. wrote to Lord Cawdor suggesting that there was nothing to stop the French using the harbour for a shelter from bad weather or 'worse purposes'. 'Give me three gunboats'. he went on, 'and thirty men moored in the Dale Roads and I could keep them out.' At least by 1814 Pembroke was fortified with a battery and two Martello towers. The former at one period had 24 guns and the latter three each. There was also a barracks, which still stands, looking over the dockyard. When built it was imperfectly octangular in form and strongly fortified with bastions at the angles, mounting heavy cannon, with numerous musket loops, 'the whole surrounded by a deep ditch. The view from this eminence is very beautiful ...'.[96]

Pembroke Dock showing one of its protective Martello towers

Thwarted by the channel and the navy, the French did succeed in landing a force in Ireland in 1798. Commanded by the capable General Humbert, a young revolutionary-trained ex-goatskin dealer and a guerilla war expert, the 1,099 men went ashore at Killala, County Mayo. On 27 August they defeated a much larger force under General Lake at the Races of Castlebar. It was a significant achievement. The Irish levies on both sides ran away and Lake's guns were captured by the bayonets of the French grenadiers. Only the rearguard fought bravely and one Fraser sentry stood

The Martello tower at the entrance to Pembroke Dock

with his back to a wall on top of some steps and shot five Frenchmen before being overpowered.[97] Humbert was master of the day, and Lake retreated. Leaving some troops behind in Castlebar, but collecting some new recruits of doubtful value, Humbert headed towards Dublin with a force numbering only 900 men. On 7 September at Ballinamuck they were confronted by Cornwallis and Lake's combined huge army of militia, highlanders and cavalry and after an hour's fighting he had to surrender. A supporting force from France of 270 men under James Napper Tandy landed at Rutland Harbour on 16 September, but left the next morning after hearing of Humbert's fate. There was to be one other attempt to lane a force in Ireland, in October 1798, but General Hardy and Wolfe Tone, who sailed in a larger fleet, ran into Admiral Warren's squadron and of their ships, all but two were captured. Amongst the captives was Wolfe Tone who later committed suicide in an Irish gaol.

In due course the French army was withdrawn from the coast and sent to Egypt where it was deprived of its transport after Nelson's victory at the Battle of the Nile. Further attempts were made to invade Britain, notably in 1803, but the main chance had been lost. A Breconshire lady wrote home from London saying: 'What dreadful times! I was glad to leave town, the preparations for an invasion is melancholy tho' necessary. They began last week to brick up the arches leading to Somerset House.'

The British fleet's final victory at Trafalgar destroyed the French and Spanish fleet and put their command of the channel, the first necessity for Napoleon if he wanted to get his barges across, completely out of the question. In 1804 the French General Dumouriez,[98] who had defected to the Allies in 1793 because he had objected to being the 'instrument of Machiavellism and oppression'. drew up detailed plans for Britain's defence. He divided the country into six military districts. Each division of 12,000 men should have 6,000 heavy infantry, 1,500 cavalry and the rest light infantry and sharpshooters as in the French army. The artillery arm was not forgotten and each battalion was to have 18 guns and two companies of mounted artillery should form the vanguard of the light infantry. The six districts were the northern counties, the Severn area, the land between the Humber and the Wash, East Anglia, the West Country, and the Home counties. Dumouriez did not consider Wales or Scotland of much importance. 'Wales is so mountainous and so poor a country,' he said, 'that the enemy would never have sufficient motive for a descent unless the possession of Ireland enabled him to recruit adherents in Wales

The defensible barracks on the hill above Pembroke Dock

and by introducing the spirit of rebellion use it as a starting point for a march upon England through Herefordshire, Monmouthshire and Gloucestershire.' He suggested strong 'places of arms' at Llandeilo, Carmarthen, Haverfordwest and Lampeter. He agreed two batteries were necessary at Fishguard but he wrote: 'it is inconceivable that the French should have selected so absurd a landing point in the absence of a call or intelligence from the inhabitants.'

Needless to say the government were polite to Doumouriez and gave him a pension of £1,000 a year but they took very little notice of his defence plans. A few schemes did, however, materialise. In south-west Wales elaborate plans for withdrawing livestock from the coast to special places inland were drawn up in Pembrokeshire and other counties. A system of beacons was arranged and Major General Gascoyne, who presided at two meetings at Haverfordwest in October 1803, ordered a monthly return on carts and carriages to be made.[99] Charles Hassall, Knox's accusor, was made Major of Pioneers and responsible for returns. Should the enemy arrive 11 guns were to be fired at St. Anne's Head which were to be answered by the same number of shots at one minute intervals in Tenby and Milford. No one suggested that this would deprive these guns from valuable stocks of powder when the time came to fire in anger.

With the mutinies at Spithead and the Nore and the troubles in Ireland it is surprising that there was no fifth column in Wales, or for that matter in England. The only suspicious event was at Plymouth where four seamen were arrested for planning to fire the powder magazines, set the French prisoners free at Keyham Point jail and raise the flag of the United Irishmen.[100] The chief plotter, Lee, said he had the support of the 58th Regiment and the crews of two men of war. He was executed with his three colleagues before any damage was done.

A silent spectator of the Spithead mutiny, Tate, was not long a prisoner. In November 1798 he was repatriated on exchange to France. He set up home with a woman friend, Genselle, at the Hotel Boston in the Rue Vivienne. Later they moved to 60 Rue Vaugirand. He had great difficulty in persuading the French Ministry to pay him his half-pay as Chef de Brigade, some 1,500 francs a year, and he soon ran into debt. It is interesting that he met Thomas Paine about this time and introduced him to Walter Savage Landor, who recorded the meeting in Tate's home during the Peace of Amiens. Landor was a wealthy young poet who later purchased Llanthony Abbey in Monmouthshire as he loved the Welsh countryside.[101] According to Landor, Paine talked about Napoleon saying that he would do harm but not for long and that he lived in terror. At this point Tate smiled and when asked why replied that his mother used to have a proverb about a frightened cat throwing down most pewter. Paine said that Napoleon would 'break his nose or bruise his cranium against every table, chair, and brick in the room until at last he must be sent to the hospital.'

'He has the finest army upon earth,' said Tate, 'and his enemies are down.' Paine, foreseeing events, said that climates and navies would destroy it. Tate called him a visionary but said Napoleon was no fool and would not throw away what he had. Paine said that he would retract his words at the first wise thing the man did. The man was all show: 'His sword, his mantle, his strut, his swagger, and even things which constitute no part of him, are his greatness; such as his porters, his guards, his soldiers, and the gilding on the ceilings of his rooms. Not those who need the fewest are the greatest but those who have the most about them are the great; as though people, like bars of iron, could be magnified and mended by adding one to the other.'

By 1809 Tate's debts forced the police to keep a dossier on him.[102] The American Ambassador, Armstrong, wrote to him about a ship leaving Dunkirk for America saying that his own family were going on her. Writing to Tone's old friend General Clarke, now Comte d'Hunebourg, Tate collected his papers, forfeited his half-pay, and went to Dunkirk. There is no further news of him, but there were Tates living at Boulogne about this time and it is possible that he never went to America. Certainly the Edouard Tate who wrote to *The Times* in 1859 (see Appendix III) must have been a relation, perhaps a nephew or a grandson. Today there is one family of Tates still in Paris but they do not profess to be any relation of the white haired, brave old man with the vivid imagination, and in later life, fund of stories, who decided that he alone should carry out what no one had achieved since the days of the Tudors: to invade Great Britain with a foreign force.

Appendix I
The Militia in June 1797, Fishguard

Commission date

Lt. Col. Comm.

    Thomas Knox   23 June 1795

Major

    William Bowen   23 June 1795

Captains

    Daniel Vaughan   18 June 1794

    Essex Bowen   23 June 1795

Lieutenants

    James Bowen   18 June 1794

    John Propert   18 June 1794

    Thomas James   21 January 1795

    William Harris   23 June, 1795

Ensigns

    David Bowen   18 June 1794

    Matthew Bowen   23 June 1795

    John Griffiths   23 June 1795

    Thomas Noot   23 June 1796

Adjutant

    James Bowen   11 July 1794

Agent, Messrs. Cox and Greenwood, Craig's Court.

Gentleman and Yeomanry, Pembroke

Captains

Richard, Lord Milford	17 July 1794
John, Lord Cawdor	31 August 1794

Lieutenants

Dudley Ackland	31 August 1794
Ch. Harris Sanxay	31 August 1794

Cornets

John Lloyd	31 August 1794
Barnet Bowen Jordan	31 August 1794

Agent, R. Croasdaile, Pulteney Street.

Pembrokeshire Militia

Lieut. Colonel

John Colby	2 January 1780

Captain

Will. Hen. Scourfield	28 Feb. 1795

Lieutenants

Thomas Jones	25 February 1780
John Freeman	14 February 1796

Ensign

Anthony J. Stokes	14 February 1796

Adjutant

Thomas Jones	4 April 1789

Quarter Master

Thomas Jones	25 January 1796

Surgeon

John Freeman	25 October 1795

Agent, Messrs. Macdonald, Bruce and Landon, Pall Mall Court.

Extracted from the Army List, Fencibles Yeomanry and Militia 1797

Appendix 2
Armée Française

Deuxieme Legion Des Francs

Etat Nominatif des Officers de la ditte Legion fait prisonnier le Sept Ventöse an 5e de la republique française, correspondant au

Etat Major Général
William Tate Général de Brigade
Française L'anhard Lieut. Aide de Camp
Nicolaus Faucon Lieut. Aide de Camp

Etat major au le Bataillon
Jes. Ple. Roch Mure (dit Le Brun) Chef de Bon.
Louis Cramer Adjut. major
Nicolas J. Leclerc Quartier maitre
Georges Nuquier Adjut. Lieutenant

Etat major du 2d Bataillon
Jean-Joseph Larose Chef de Bon.
Pierre Dams Adjut. major
Pierre Chevalier Quartier maitre
Georges Nuquier Adjut. Lieutenant

Jn Bte. Beutoh Adjut. Lieutenant (Il etté malade à h'tal)
Jean Baptiste Larand Chirugien Major

Capitaines
Aute Marie Didier; Pierre Bertrand; Louis Garde; Nicolas Tyrell [spelled Tayrelle on the document, which appears to be written by Tate himself]; Pierre Paul Gilsero; Robert Morrison; Louis Verneuil; Francois Gambart Larnelle; Jn. Bte. Caillot; Jn. Chamerlot; Jacques Eustache; Charles Auguste Tanerel.

Lieutenants
Jean Hubert Gaspard; Henry Cabiste St. Marc; Etienne Bailly; Renée Gourreau; Joseph Deloisy; Jean Pajeot; Mathias Morwelch; Jn. Bte. Paviot; Etienne Simphurin Joby; Antoine Sanglet; Barry St. Leger; Antoine Rochelle.

Sous Lieutenants
Jn. Bte. Derousseau; Pierre Béjin; Pierre Michel; Pierre Selandaih; Francois Deban; Jaques Philipe Felix Geuzo; Jean Mongin; Georges Pre. Guerinet; Jean Camerel; Gabriel Mervile; Andre Drouet; Nicolas Mainat.

On another document, signed by Hoche, there is a list indicating that the French were divided into twelve troops, each with three officers, a Sgt. Major, two sergeants, one corporal (*fourier*, i.e. in charge of rations), four ordinary corporals, and a drummer. Two of these troops were grenadiers. Barry St. Leger, whose account of the affair implies he was the most active of all the officers, was serving under Captain Eustache.

The composition of the French troops, which is preserved on a document in the Carmarthen County Archives is given as: 200 'Chouans' (an abbreviation of chat-huant, or owl. They were the 'night birds' who fought for the Vendée before changing sides when captured) 400 republicans and 564 deserters, Paris gaol-birds, émigrés and other criminals, some of whom were in chains when they embarked.

The total was 1,194 men and 35 officers, two officers' wives and two soldiers' wives, making a grand total of 1,233. However Hoche's document could have been prepared before the fleet sailed and all accounts point to the French party being larger than 1,233.

Appendix 3

Alexander Ridgway wrote to *The Times* on 23 December, 1859 saying that the French plundering led to their capture and the Charming Welshes were largely responsible for Tate's surrender. He says he still has the sword of his grandfather (Second Lieut. Thomas Ridgway of the Pembroke Volunteers) at 3 Fitzroy Square and finishes by stating: 'I number among my relations a quiet English parson with a large family, grandson of a French officer who then became a prisoner of war and plundered a Welsh squire of his daughter's heart.'

Letter published in *The Times* on 27 December 1859, signed by Edouard Tate, Leicester Square, two days earlier.

Although I feel that enough has been written on this trivial subject, I confess I should like to show Mr. Ridgway who writes not very politely, how worthless are the grandmamma's tales which he seeks to impose upon you and upon the hon. public as history. At first I will observe that my own statement is not founded on any French authority, nor is it founded on the exaggerated recollections or predilections of any of my own family; it is wholly founded on the English Official Account of the transaction, and on the justificative pieces attached to that account, with which it entirely agrees.

Lord Cawdor, whom I erroneously styled 'Count' a title I am informed you don't have in England, states that the French commenced to land on the morning of the 23rd February and that before 10pm of the same day they had landed, had written to his Lordship offering to surrender and had had their offer accepted. This allows very few hours indeed for the perpetration of all the outrages which are imputed to them.

According to Lord Cawdor, although the French wrote to him offering to surrender early on the 23rd, the frigates which had conveyed them did not weigh anchor until late that evening. According to the tradition of Mr. Ridgway's grandparents, the French surrendered because their frigates were driven off the coast by bad weather.

Mr. Ridgway further discloses that it was Mr. Tate's messenger bearing the letter offering to surrender and not Mr. Tate himself, who is supposed to have been imposed upon by the red petticoats of the Welshes and the various uniforms of the volunteers. But, as the letter must have been written before the messenger could carry it, it is difficult to imagine how the offer which it contained could have been extorted by the fears inspired by the aspect of gentlemen and ladies in red attire who had never been seen even by the messenger at the time it was written.

Finally and I beg attention to this as it proves how little Mr. Ridgway really knows about the subject upon which he seeks to correct me and enlighten you, we are told by that gentleman that 'Squire Campbell of Fishguard was subsequently called upon by the British Government to wear an Earl's coronet as a reward for the latent military capacity which he discovered in capturing Mr. Tate and his men.'

Now an obliging friend has pointed out to me that Burke's Peerage (a reliable authority he assures me) indicates that Mr. Campbell of Stackpole Court, long Member of Parliament for Cardigan, was raised to the peerage as Baron Cawdor of Castlemartin on 21 June, 1796 eight months before Mr. Tate set foot in Wales and that he never wore an Earl's coronet at all.

Appendix 4
The Ships

The French ship *Minerva* was captured in 1794 off San Fiorenzo, Corsica, and was re-named *Saint Fiorenzo* after the place she was captured as there was already a *Minerva* in the navy at the time.

La Nymphe. The first ship of this name, a sloop, was burnt at Tortola in 1783 'through the carelessness of the Purser's steward.' The second, the ship with which we are concerned, was captured from the French in 1780. The ship took some time to repair after her capture by the *Flora* and later served as a 36-gun frigate, Captain E. Pellew, with distinction. When in action against *La Constance* and *La Résistance* her captain was John Cooke. She saw service for 30 years until finally wrecked in a storm.

Fisgard. *La Résistance* was renamed after the event in which she was concerned and the old spelling was used. She served in many engagements and her captain Byam Martin, later an Admiral, fought and captured the French *Immortalité* in 1798, one of the ships that took Wolfe Tone's expedition to Ireland. In 1800 she took part in a daring attack on Corunna and in 1804 she helped in the blockade of Toulon. In 1809 with a new captain, William Bolton, she helped capture Curaçao from the Dutch and was grounded at St. Anne harbour for a time during the early part of the action. In 1809 she took part in the Walcheren expedition under the Earl of Chatham. A new *Fisgard* was launched in 1819 at Pembroke and christened by Lord Cawdor, when the old one had been sold out of the navy. She later became the Commodore's ship at Woolwich and remained until 1879. During the First World War various ships at Portsmouth comprised *HMS Fisguard*, a training establishment for engine-room artificers. One of them, formerly the *Invincible*, foundered off Portland in 1914 and sunk with the loss of 21 lives. Today the *Fisgard* is the training establishment at Torpoint, Plymouth for boy artificers and is a shore station.

La Constance. She kept her own name and joined the navy as a 6th rate. In October 1806 she ran aground off Brittany and was recaptured by the French and taken to St. Malo. Her captain, Alexander S. Burrowes, was killed in the action.

(Information supplied by Capt. T. D. Manning, CBE, RNVR, joint author of *British Warship Names*, London 1966).

Appendix 5
Will of William Tate

I William Tate of South Carolina Seriously considering the uncertainty of human life in the best do while in a sound state of mind make this my last will and Testament Intending to dispose of all my worldly affairs not as humour may prompt but as justice and equity seem to direct

I most humbly recommend my Soul to the extensive mercy of that Eternal Supreme Intelligint being who gave it me I give devise and bequeath unto my Nephew William Tate son of my oldest Brother Samuel Tate of the Kingdom of Iriland Two thirds of all my Estate both Real and personal forever I give devise and bequeath unto my beloved Wife Elizabeth Tate in lieu of all her Dower One third part of all my Estate both Real and personal during her natural life and at her decease to my above mentioned Nephew William Tate of the Kingdom of Ireland and lastly I appoint my good and Trusty Friends John Chestnut and Zachariah Canty Executors to this my last Will and Testament

Signed Camden the Twelfth day of September in the year of our lord One thousand Seven hundred and Eighty Seven

    In the presince of
    William Brown
    John Kershaw   Wm. Tate (Seal)
    Zach Canty
    Recorded in Will Book C. Page 77
    Recorded July 30th 1792
    Francis Boykin C.C.
    Apt. 66. Pkg. 2357.

Bibliography

Aspinall, A. *Later correspondence of George III*. Cambridge, 1956.

Brown, J. *History of Haverfordwest*. Brigstocke, 1914.

Bonnechose, E. Lazare *Hoche*. Paris, 1867.

Curtis, M. *Antiquities of Laugharne, Pendine and their neighbour hoods ...* London, 1880.

Davies, D. Rev. *The Influence of the French Revolution on Welsh Life and Literature.* Carmarthen, 1926.

Douglas, Sylvester. *Diaries.* London, 1901.

Edwards, Averyl and Davies, Sir L.T. *Welsh Life in the 18th Century*. London, 1939.

Evans, Thomas. *The Background of Modern Welsh Politics 1789–1846*. Cardiff, 1936.

Fenton, Richard. *A historical tour through Pembrokeshire*. Brecon, 1903.

Fortescue, The Hon. Sir John. *History of the British Army*. Vol. IV. London, 1906.

Heitman, F.B. *Historical Register of Officers of the Continental Army during the War of the Revolution*. Washington, 1914.

Hemphill, W.E. *Extracts from the journal of the Provincial Congress of South Carolina, 1775–76*. U.S.C. Press, 1967.

Inglis-Jones, E. *Peacocks in Paradise*. London, 1968.

James, Miss M.E. *The Fishguard Invasion or Three Days in 1797*. Cardiff, 1897.

James, William. *Naval History of Great Britain*. Vol. II. London, 1860.

John, B.S. *The Fishguard and Pembroke Area*. Sheffield, 1972.

Knox, Thomas. *Some account of the proceedings that took place on the landing of the French near Fishguard ...* London, 1800.

Laird Clowes, Sir W. *The Royal Navy: A History*. Vols. IV and V. London, 1899–1900.

Laws, Edward. *Little England Beyond Wales*. London, 1888.

Lefebyre, G. *The Directory* (Translation). London, 1966.

MacDermot, F. *Theobald Wolfe Tone*. London, 1906.

Madelin, L. *La France du Directoire Paris*, 1934.

Mahan, A.T. *The Influence of Sea Power on the French Revolution and Empire* Vol I. London, 1893.

Mason, R.A *Guide to Milford Haven and the Vicinity*. Tenby, 1860?

Maurice, J.W. Rev. *History of the French Invasion near Fishguard*. Fishguard, 1911.

Miller, J. C. Alexander Hamilton. *Portrait in Paradox*.

Minningerode, Meade *Jefferson, Friend of France*. New York, 1928. New York, 1959.

Mirehouse, M.B. *South Pembrokeshire*. London, 1910.

Naval Record Society: Spencer Papers, Vol. 1. London, 1913.

Pakenham, Thomas. The Year of Liberty. London, 1969.

Pearson, Hesketh. *Tom Paine, Friend of Mankind*. London, 1937.

Pugh, Maj. Gen. L.H.O., C.B., C.B.E., D.S.O. *History of the Pembroke Yeomanry*. Haverfordwest, 1969.

Richmond, Admiral Sir H.W. *The Invasion of Britain*. London, 1941.

Rogers, F. *Evolution of a Federalist*. U.S.C. Press, 1962

Rose, J.H. and Broadley, A.M. *Dumouriez and the Defence of England Against Napoleon*. London, 1908.

Rutland, Duke of. *Journal of a tour through North and South Wales*. London, 1805.

Slater, Isaac. *Royal National Commercial Directory and Topography of Wales*. 1858.

Stuart Jones, Cmdr. E.H. *The Last Invasion of Britain*. Cardiff, 1950.

Tone, W.T.W. (editor) *Life of Theobald Wolfe Tone*. Washington, 1826.

Vaughan-Thomas, Wynford and Llewellyn, Alun. *The Shell Guide to Wales*. London, 1969.

Wheeler, H.F.B. and Broadley, A.M. *Napoleon and the Invasion of England*. London, 1908.

Williams, D. *The Rebecca Riots*. Cardiff, 1971.

Williams, D., *History of Modern Wales*. London, 1951.

Williams, H.L. (Ap Gwilym, H.L.) *An authentic account of the Invasion by the French ... on 22nd February*, 1797. 2nd edition. Haverfordwest, 1853.

Journals and unpublished papers

American Historical Review, Vol. X, 1896.

Annual Register, 1797.

Cawdor Papers at Carmarthenshire County Record Office.

Cymmrodorion Society Transactions:

       Harries of Tregwynt 1944/45

       Some farmers of bygone Pembrokeshire 1944/45

       The French Invasion of Pembrokeshire 1932

       The Vaughans of Golden Grove 1966(1)

Daily Telegraph Colour Supplement, 225, January, 1969.

Felix Farley's Bristol Journal, 1797.

Jones, Major F., T.D., D.L., M.A., F.S.A., Unpublished MS on Cawdor Family.

Journal of the Army Historical Research Society, Vol. 6., 1927.

Letters in *The Fishguard County Echo*, 25 June, 1936, 8 December, 1932.

Log book of *San Fiorenzo*, National Maritime Museum Library.

National Library of Wales Journal, Vol. VI, 303, 1969.

Quarterly Review, April, 1935.

Salmon Papers at Pembroke County Library.

Stowe Papers at Henry E. Huntingdon Museum, California.

The Bath Herald, 1797

The Moniteur, 1797 (An. V)

The Times, 1797 and letters of 27 Dec. 1859, 21 Dec. 1859.

The Welsh History Review Vol. 6, Dec. 1972 (2).

West Wales Historical Review, Vol. XIV, 1929.

Endnotes

Note: WWHR — West Wales Historical Review. THSC — Transactions of the Honourable Society of Cymmrodorion. Books not in the Bibliography have been referred to in full.

Prologue
1. Bryant. *The Years of Endurance.*
2. Evans. *The Background of Modern Welsh Politics.*
3. *Ibid.*

The Militia
4. Clode. *Military Forces of the Crown.*
5. Pictures and uniform at the Haverfordwest H.Q. of 'A' Troop, 227 Squadron RCT (Pembroke Yeomanry). Lt. Col. Howells and Capt. The Hon. T. Lewis of the Yeomanry have designed their own dress uniforms for present day use.
6. Buckinghamshire County Record Office, Militia Papers.
7. Henry E. Huntingdon Library, California. Stowe Papers.
8. *Felix Farley's Bristol Journal*, Feb. 1797.
9. Brown: *The Rise, Progress and Military Improvement of the Bristol Volunteers.*
10. Dropmore Papers, Vol. III.

Fishguard
11. John, B.S. *The Fishguard and Pembroke Area* Geographical Arch. 1972.
12. Davies and Edwards. *Welsh Life in the 18th Century.*
13. THSC 1943/44: *Some Farmers of Bygone Pembrokeshire.*
14. Davies and Edwards. *Welsh Life in the 18th Century.*

The French Plan
15. Nicolay. *Napoleon at the Boulogne Camp.*
16. Parson and White. *History, Directory and Gazeteer of the Counties of Durham and Northumberland* Vol. II. (1828)
17. Wheeler and Broadley. *Napoleon and the Invasion of Britain.*
18. Rogers. *Evolution of a Federalist*, Charlston 1962.
19. Letter to author from South Carolina Historical Society.
20. *American Historical Review.* Vol. X. Footnote.
21. Minnigerode Meade. *Jefferson Friend of France.*
22. Miller, J.C. *Alexander Hamilton: Portrait in Paradox.*
23. Tone: *Life of Theobald Wolfe Tone.*

Invasion

24. James. *The History of the Navy*. Vol. II.
25. Letter from A.S. Cutliffe, Chairman Ilfracombe Museum Trustees.
26. *Daily Telegraph Magazine* No. 225. Article by J.B.H. Peel based on the notes made on the French despatches.
27. Warburton. *History of Solva*.
28. W/O: 10/308.
29. Gwilym. *An authentic account of the Invasion by the French on 22nd February 1797*. 2nd ed. Haverfordwest (1853).

The Battle that didn't take place

30. Fenton. *A Historical Tour through Pembrokeshire*.
31. Knox. *Some account etc*.
32. Information from Lt. Cmdr. Burrington-Harries.
33. Knox. *op. cit*.
34. *Ibid*.
35. Information from Mrs. Perkins.
36. Warburton. *op. cit*.
37. *Fishguard County Echo*. 8.12.32.
38. THSC 1966. 1. *The Vaughans of Golden Grove*.

The Surrender and Trials

39. *News and Notes*. Nat. Lib. of Wales 1950. p.303.
40. Salmon Notebook. Pem. County Library.
41. Stuart Jones. *The Last Invasion of Britain*.
42. *Annual Register*, 1797.
43. Gwilym. *op. cit*. Some accounts attribute this to Cawdor but Gwilym's account is verified by two Fencibles, Peter Davies and Owen Griffiths, who may well have overheard the remark.
44. WWHR. Vol. XIV.
45. Cawdor Papers.
46. Maurice. *The Fishguard Invasion*.
47. WWHR *op. cit*.
48. *Ibid*.
49. Cawdor Papers.
50. WWHR. *op. cit*
51. Information from Mrs. Perkins, whose ancestor led the naval ratings.
52. Salmon Notebook. *op. cit*.
53. Knox. *Some account etc*.
54. The muskets are all flint locks, marked with the revolutionary symbol, barrels 3ft. 7in., total length varies from 4ft. 10in. to 5ft., weight 9½lbs. The bayonets, of which one survives in Tenby museum, are ring type with a small supporting lug. Each musket has two brass bands and swivels for slings. An NCO's sword in the museum has the words Cassagnard, Fourbisseur du Roy au Nantes and the Sun, Moon and Stars engraved on both sides. The hilt is very plain.

55. WWHR. *op. cit.*
56. Cawdor Papers.
57. Maurice. *op. cit.*
58. *Ibid.*
59. THSC Vol. XLIII 1932.
60. Stuart Jones. *op. cit.*
61. Family history.
62.
63. Knox. *op. cit.*
64. *Fishguard County Echo,* 25.6.36. John's son served in the Royal Bucks Militia later on and the name Macnamara appears in the Bucks Militia Book.
65. Cawdor Papers.
66. The officers are Lord Cawdor, Capt. Pem. Yeo. Cavalry; Lieut. Dudley Ackland; Acting Cornet Jos. Adams; Capt. Scourfield; Capt. Edwards; Capt. Bowen; Cornet Bowling; Capt. R. Foley; Lieut. Roche; Lieut. Harries; Cornet Barret Jordan; Surgeon Voyle; Lieut. Feale; Lieut. W. Bowen; Lieut. E. W. Jones; Capt. Ackland; Lieut. Lord; 2nd Lieut. Thos. Ridgway. (See Appendix 3).
67. Cawdor Papers.
68. WWHR. *op. cit*
69. WWHR. *op. cit*
70. Cawdor Papers.
71. Lord Cawdor's 1797 diary is unfortunately missing from the Cawdor Papers but as it is quoted by Stuart Jones, he must have been the last to see it when he wrote his book in 1950.
72. WWHR. *op. cit*
73. Salmon Notebook.
74. *Moniteur.* An. V. 6.3.1797.
75. Letter from George Bowen. Nat. Lib. of Wales No. 13460.

The Prisoners & Further Alarms
76. Stuart Jones. *op. cit.*
77. Cawdor Papers.
78. Laws. *Little England Beyond Wales.*
79. Cawdor Papers.
80. Rutland, Duke of. *op. cit.*
81. *Pembrokeshire Antiquities.*
82. Cawdor Papers.
83. *Ibid.*
84. Inglis-Jones. *Peacocks in Paradise.*
85. Cawdor Papers.
86. Stuart Jones. *op. cit.*
87. *Arch. Cam* 1881 p.88
88. THSC 1867. 1. *The Society of Sea Serjeants.*

Results in London & Elsewhere

89. Douglas, Sylvester (Lord Glenbervie) *Diaries*.
90. Cawdor Papers.
91. Aspinall. *Later Correspondence of George III*.
92. *Hansard* 1797
93. Namier and Brooke. *The Commons 1754–90* HMSO 1964.
94. Vol. LXVIII
95. Lloyd. *Historical Memoranda of Breconshire* Vol. I. Brecon 1903.
96. *Mason's Guide to Milford Haven and the Vicinity*.
97. Grant. *British Battles on Land and Sea* Vol. II.
98. Rose and Broadley. *Dumouriez and the Defence of England Against Napoleon*.
99. WWHR. Vol. XIV.
100. Duggan. *The Great Mutiny*.
101. Pearson. *Tom Paine, Friend of Mankind*.
102. Fleming P. *Invasion 1940*. London 1958.

Index of Persons

Around & About South-West Wales
by Graham Roberts, 288 pages, 300 photographs, £12.95

This book comprises ten road-based tours ranging from 25 to 100 miles in length that cover Pembrokeshire, Cardiganshire, Carmarthenshire, parts of Glamorgan and a large part of Powys. Starting from seven different localities the tours cover a range of spectacular scenery, many well and less well known historically or architecturally interesting buildings, several towns, a good handful of villages, many beaches, a clutch of prehistoric sites, gardens open to the public, nature reserves and much besides. Developed from a knowledge of the area gained over many years, the tours will lead you to places which you would otherwise have needed time to find out about as visitors — even some long-standing local residents may be surprised and carried away by what they have missed out on seeing to date.

Castles and Bishops Palaces of Pembrokeshire
by Lise Hull, 238 pages, over 100 photographs and plans, £7.95

Introductory chapters detail the history of the arrival of the Normans and Welsh response which saw the initial construction of the castles, the destruction of some and ever strengthening of others. A gazetteer then covers the 69 castles and bishops palaces in the county, form the lowliest motte to the great castles such as Carew, Cilgerran, Haverfordwest, Manorbier and Pembroke.

Pembrokeshire: a year and a day
a photographic exploration of the county, 144 pages
with 125 mainly colour photographs. Hardback £20, paperback £12.95

Eleven photographers have come together to provide a mix of images that show Pembrokeshire in its stunning beauty in a range of light and across the seasons. Portrayed are numerous of the county's bays, stretches of the coast-line, several historic sites, occasional remnants of the industrial past, sporting activities, the Preseli hills, the Gwaun valley and much flora. Some of the photographs are taken from the air, and one dangling from a rope. The quality of images is undeniable and several will cause pause for thought.